To

With ...

Buddy

April 2002

JAPANESE-AMERICAN

VETERANS

OF

MINNESOTA

by

Edwin M. Nakasone

Japanese American Veterans of Minnesota
Printed in the United States of America

Publisher's Cataloging in Publication Data

Nakasone, Edwin M.
  Japanese American Verterans of Minnesota.
  1st ed.
     204 p.   ill.   23cm.
  Includes foreward and preface.
  ISBN 1-930922-02-7 (pbk.)
  1. World War, 1939-1945--Participation, Japanese
American.   2. World War, 1939-1945--Japanese American--
personal narratives.   3. Korean War, 1950-1953--Japanese
American--Personal narratives.   4. Japan--history--Allied
occupation, 1945-1952--Personal narratives.   5. Japanese
American Veterans of Minnesota.   6. Japanese American
Veterans--Personal narratives. I. Title.
D753.8 .N35 2002
940.53/089

Published by **j**-Press Publishing
4796 N. 126th St.
White Bear Lake, MN 55110
Phone: 888-407-1723 Fax: 651-429-1819
email: sjackson@jpresspublishing.com
Web: http://www.jpresspublishing.com

This book is dedicated to:

All Nikkei veterans and supporters of the
Japanese American veterans of Minnesota

and to

Daniel

David and Joseph

JAPANESE AMERICAN

VETERANS

OF

MINNESOTA

CAMP SAVAGE

During World War II, some 5,000-6,000 Japanese-American soldiers, members of the U.S. Army's Military Intelligence Service, were given intensive and accelerated classes in the Japanese language at Camp Savage.

Their subsequent work translating captured documents, maps, battle plans, diaries, letters, and printed materials and interrogating Japanese prisoners made them "Our human secret weapons," according to President Harry Truman, who commended them following the war.

The Military Intelligence Service (MIS) program began in the fall of 1941, a few weeks before Pearl Harbor, at the Presidio in San Francisco.

For security reasons it was moved in May, 1942 to Camp Savage, a site personally selected by language school commandant Colonel Kai E. Rasmussen, who believed Savage was "a community that would accept Japanese Americans for their true worth—American soldiers fighting with their brains for their native America."

The 132-acre site had served as a Civilian Conservation Corps camp in the 1930s and was later used to house elderly indigent men.

Conditions there were extremely difficult in the early months of the war, when the first students studied without desks, chairs, or even beds. By August, 1944 the program had outgrown Camp Savage and was moved to larger facilities at Fort Snelling.

Most of the English-speaking Japanese Americans, known as Nisei, were from the West Coast area. Some were already in the U.S. military service when they were selected for the language school, while others were volunteers from the camps in which American citizens of Japanese ancestry had been interned following the bombing of Pearl Harbor.

According to General Charles Willoughby, chief of intelligence for General Douglas MacArthur, "the 6,000 Nisei shortened the Pacific war by two years."

ERECTED BY THE
SAVAGE CHAMBER OF COMMERCE
1993

Camp Savage Memorial Monument

CONTENTS

Foreword, Page 10
Preface, Page 14
Chapter One, Toshio W. Abe. Page 28
Chapter Two, Tom T. Ohye, Page 39
Chapter Three, Dr. George T. Tani, Page 48
Chapter Four, Minoru Yoshida, Page 55
Chapter Five, Harry Tsutomu Umeda, Page 58
Chapter Six, Mitsuso Yoneji, Page 74
Chapter Seven, Isamu Sugimoto, Page 82
Chapter Eight, Hisashi Kumagai, Page 88
Chapter Nine, Edwin M. Nakasone, Page 93
Chapter Ten, Isamu Shimada, Page 109
Chapter Eleven, Isamu Saito, Page 113
Chapter Twelve, Toke Yonekawa, Page 118
Chapter Thirteen, Akira Fujioka, Page 123
Chapter Fourteen, Paul Shimizu, Page 132
Chapter Fifteen, Osamu Honda, Page 142
Chapter Sixteen, Tom Ohno, Page 152
Chapter Seventeen, David Yahanda, Page 159
Chapter Eighteen, Conclusion, Page 163
Photos: Other JAVM Members, Page 165
Photos: Old Camp Savage, Page 167
Photos: Old Fort Snelling, Page168
Photos: JAVM Meetings & Luncheons, Page 173
Photos: JAVM Memorial Day Service, Page 174

FOREWORD

This *Japanese American Veterans of Minnesota* (JAVM) book of memories is long overdue. It has been an ongoing project of the editor for over five years. JAVM itself has not had a long history. JAVM traces its beginnings to 1991 when a strong call and push came from the Southern California Military Intelligence Service Club for the Minnesota veterans to host a Military Intelligence Service Language School (MISLS) "sentimental journey" reunion. It had been fifty years since Camp Savage, Minnesota had opened its rustic buildings for the task of training Japanese linguists in the MISLS.

JAVM was not formally organized then. We were but a small group of MIS veterans and we declined to undertake the huge task of organizing and hosting the event which would eventually draw up to 400 MIS veterans and spouses nationwide. Yet, the Southern California club would not accept our rationale of insufficient manpower and offered to help monetarily, administratively and logistically. When many of us still remained negative and greatly reluctant to sponsor a national reunion, a shining star appeared. This was Mrs. Grace Ohama. She, along with her daughter, Kathy Ohama Koch, began planning the events. Inspired by her confidence the JAVM vets organized and with Bill Doi and Tom Moriguchi (deceased) as co-chairs, various committees were formed. Spouses and friends pitched in whole heartedly and a very successful "sentimental journey" reunion took place in Minneapolis in May 1992. Congressman Norman Mineta (D-CA) was the keynote speaker.

JAVM members received sincere accolades from everyone attending the reunion and it can be said that our reunion served as a model for all future national MIS reunions. The reunion organizing efforts convinced all of us of the great need for a Minnesota Nikkei veterans organization. Soon thereafter, a meeting was convened to organize, and given the small number of MIS vets in Minnesota and the close social bonds held with other Nikkei veterans, such as those of the 100th Infantry Battalion, and the 442nd Regimental Combat Team, as well as those who participated in the Korean War, Vietnam War and the Occupation periods, it was unanimously decided to invite all such people to join the Japanese American Veterans of Minnesota organization. We were able to recruit about twenty five members.

Officers of JAVM to the present are, Edwin (Bud) Nakasone (president,) O. Sam Honda (Vice president,) and Kathy O. Koch (Secretary Treasurer.)

THE NEED FOR A BOOK

It is common knowledge that veterans of the second World War are fast disappearing. All are in their seventies, eighties, or even nineties, and thousands of the eight million plus men, "The Greatest Generation," as termed by author Tom Brokaw, are dying daily. Niseis, a unique body of veterans because of their ethnicity, are likewise dying. In the last few years we have lost a good number of Minnesota Nisei veterans. It was therefore the editor's desire to capture the memories and stories of the Minnesota Nikkei veterans. As is the national propensity of veterans, AJAs (Americans of Japanese ancestry), generally, find it extremely difficult to "open up" and discuss their military service experiences. When asked to write or respond to oral interviews or inquiries, the common retort was "aw, I don't have any war stories," or "I'm no hero so I don't want to have others know about my stories." At present, JAVM has a membership of approximately twenty five members, and despite the *enryo* cultural trait of AJAs, I was able to interview and put into print the experiences of seventeen members.

Perseverance or the spirit of "*gambare*" encouraged me, as the editor, to keep on pursuing the veterans. It is of the utmost importance for our children and grandchildren to know how the sacrifices and courageous efforts of the Nisei generation fostered the present climate of Japanese

American acceptance within the main social stream of America. With so many of our present day offspring not knowledgeable of our Japanese heritage, the sacrifices made, the legacies achieved, I felt that it was imperative to pursue and publish the activities and deeds of our Minnesota AJA veterans. Even in the academic world or history textbooks one hardly discovers worthy and heartfelt appreciation of our W.W.II efforts, and so I'm hopeful that published materials of this genre will evoke the attention of the American public. It is with these aims that this book has been published and the editor hopes it will aid readers to understand and appreciate the contributions of AJAs to Minnesota and America.

PREFACE

It is well noted that more than 6,000 Niseis served the US Army as linguists during W.W.II and were credited by MacArthur's chief of intelligence, Major General Charles Willoughby, as having shortened the Pacific war by at least two years. President Harry Truman commented on the work of the Niseis as "our human secret weapons." Minnesota's Nikkei of today, for the most part, can trace their Minnesota roots to Camp Savage and Fort Snelling.

As war appeared imminent in 1941, the US. War

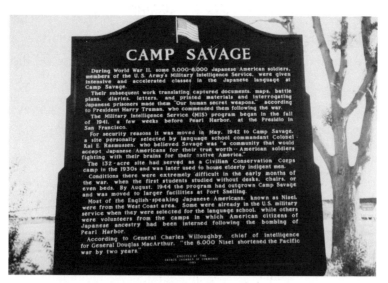

Camp Savage, Savage, Minnesota, was the site of the military Intelligence Service Language School (May, 1942-Aug., 1944). The School next moved to Fort Snelling, Minnesota, Aug, 1944-July, 1946.

Department, cognizant of the complex Japanese language, made a hurried search to discover American soldiers or citizens who were Japanese language experts or who could be trained to master

The only remaining building from the wartime Camp Savage, home of the MISLS. Today the building houses state transportation department equipment.

the language. The results were dismal, only a handful. It was at this juncture that the army "discovered" Niseis—did they not speak Japanese and attend Japanese schools over and beyond the English public schools? Subsequent surveys yielded fifty eight (58) eligible Nisei soldiers, and the first class in Japanese was started by the Fourth US Army headquarters in the Presidio of San Francisco. This first class consisted of two *hakujin* (Caucasian) and fifty eight Nisei soldiers, a total of 60 students. The faculty consisted of six Nisei civilian educators. The school's budget was only $2,000 and they were given an abandoned hangar at Crissey Field on the base as their school building. All equipment, papers, desks, typewriters, chairs, etc. were necessarily scrounged from the main post. The instructors hurriedly

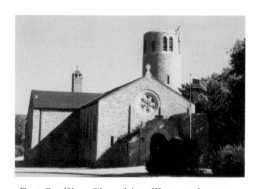

Fort Snelling Chapel is still operating as a nondenominational Christian church. Many MIS veterans worshiped there and some were even married in this beautiful chapel.

made their own teaching texts since none were available in the army supply system. The school was opened on 1 November, 1941.

With the attack on Pearl Harbor on 7 December 1941, and President Roosevelt's Executive Order 9066, dated 19 February, 1942, the school could not remain in California and had to be moved inland. Colonel Kai Rasmussen, who was the commandant, traveled throughout the United States, seeking a community that would accept Japanese Americans "for their true worth— American soldiers fighting with their brains for their native America." Almost everywhere Colonel

Company C (foreground) and Company F (beyond pine tree) are still evident though unoccupied since the Veterans Administration left many years ago.

Rasmussen searched, the usual response was "No way, we don't want any Japs in our neighborhood." But Minnesota's Governor Harold Stassen offered the former Civilian Conservation Corps and Old Men's Home, a 132 acre site, to the War Department, and Rasmussen graciously accepted saying, "There is not a place in the country where the school could have been run so successfully." Later, he remarked, "The twin cities accorded the friendliest treatment to Nisei students and have made them welcome." "The War Department," he said, "is extremely grateful for the cooperation displayed by people of these communities." Meanwhile, the San Francisco class of 60 had graduated and except for fifteen of them, who were held back as NCO instructors, the rest were sent into the Pacific war.

The first class of Camp Savage then began in May 1942. According to JAVM member Tosh Abe, "the camp was inadequate, filthy, and we had to clean up the buildings and set up the classrooms, barracks, mess hall, latrines, everything." Harry Umeda commented, "We were the first bunch to arrive and we didn't even have a bed to sleep on. We had to sleep on mattresses on the floor—we had no desks or chairs in the classroom."

Yet, as the Pacific war continued ferociously, more and more urgent requests came in for MISLS trained graduates. Classroom training continued unabated, Mondays through Friday from 0730 in the morning to 2100 in the evening, with time off for meals. Dr. George Tani remembered studying after "lights out" under his blanket with a flashlight, and "many went to the lighted latrines to study." George also remembered that "in the cold winter days we were permitted to wear knitted masks over our faces."

The MIS linguists were all over the Pacific and Asiatic theater of operations. Be it the Attu and Kiska campaigns, Australia, the Solomons, the Carolines (Makin and Tarawa,) the Marshalls (Kwajalein and Eniwetok,) the China, Burma, India (CBI) campaigns, New Guinea, Mariannas (Saipan, Tinian, Guam,) the Philippines, Okinawa; the MIS linguists were there saving lives and ensuring victory for America. Praiseworthy were their language skills which were instrumental in our victories at Midway, the shooting down of Admiral Yamamoto's plane over New Britain Island, and the American naval air fleet's destruction of Japan's air arm during the battle of the Philippine Sea in June 1944. The Nisei linguists were key to these victories with their radio intercepts, translations, and by communicating the import of their radio intercepts to higher headquarters immediately.

With continued calls for more MIS linguists, Camp Savage could no longer house, maintain, and service the increasing number of Nisei soldiers coming in for schooling. Fortunately, larger, permanent facilities were located at Fort Snelling in St. Paul, and so the school was moved into

18

this facility in August, 1944. By the end of the war and close thereafter, more than 6,000 Nisei soldiers had graduated from the Military Intelligence Service Language School. MISLS was then moved to the Presidio of Monterey, California, in July of 1946. So, Camp Savage and Fort Snelling provided the necessary welcome, acceptance and approval, as well as their magnificent language training, which provided the impetus for the Nisei soldiers to accomplish their valued and heroic deeds.

Membership within JAVM is small in number and with the close social bonds developed through the years of hardy Minnesota living, it was decided early on to invite all Japanese American veterans to join the organization, with spouses and friends, to be associate members.

Historical Background

The following stories highlight our 100th/442nd veterans.

The 100th Infantry Battalion was originally composed of Hawaii Niseis who were conscripted prior to the war. They were on duty in Hawaii with the federalized Hawaii National Guard Regiments, the 298th Infantry and the 299th Infantry when Pearl Harbor was attacked. Shortly thereafter all soldiers of Japanese ancestry were placed in a provisional Hawaii battalion and did supernumerary (euphemism for labor) duties. Disappointment, anger, sadness and lowered morale ran rampant among the 1,432 soldiers

Fortunately, the Hawaiian Department Army Commander, Lieutenant General Delos C. Emmons, respected and believed in their Americanism, the loyalty, spirit and vitality of these soldiers and recommended to the War Department in January 1942, to have these men train as combat infantry men on the mainland. They were shipped to the mainland and were soon given the colors of the 100th Infantry Battalion (Separate) and began their infantry training at Camp McCoy, Wisconsin, in March 1942. They took as their motto, "Remember Pearl Harbor." Six months later they were receiving their advanced combat training at Camp Shelby, Mississippi, and proved themselves as superior infantry men during the long Louisiana maneuvers in the fall of 1942. They sailed for Oran, Algeria and were attached to the 34th Division at Oran, Algeria. This was in September 1943.

From Algeria they sailed to Italy and in September 1943, the 100th received their baptism of fire in Salerno, Italy. They fought their way up the Italian peninsula from Montemarano, Benevento, across the Volturno River, through San Angelo d'Alife, around Castle Hill and Monte Cassino, across the Rapido River and joined the 442nd RCT at Civitaveccia on 11 June 1944. The 100th was allowed to keep its designation as the 100th Battalion even as it became the lst Battalion of the normal three battalion organization of a regiment. The extremely heavy losses suffered by the 100th earned it the brave monicker of the "Purple Heart Battalion."

The men of the 100th through 18 months of combat lost 337 men, won three Presidential Unit Citations, earned 1,703 Purple Hearts, one Medal of Honor, 24 Distinguished Service Crosses, 147 Silver Stars, 2,713 Bronze Stars, and 30 Division Commendations.

442nd Regimental Combat Team

The superb record of the 100th Infantry Battalion, the continued requests of the AJA and other civilian leaders in Hawaii, the Japanese American Citizens League and Lieutenant General Delos C. Emmons, Hawaiian Department Commander convinced President Franklin D. Roosevelt and the War Department to issue a call of volunteers for army service. This was on 28 January 1943. On the mainland, due to their incarceration in concentration camps where their personal freedoms had been quashed, and due to the War Relocation Authority's insensitive loyalty questionnaire, only 1,181 volunteered; many were heavily criticized and ostracized by other internees. The War Department had assigned a quota of 3,000 originally to the mainlanders.

In Hawaii, where no general incarceration had occurred,

over 11,000 men volunteered and this astounded army and government authorities. Hawaii's original quota was set at 1,500. They had not been victimized like their mainland Nisei counterparts and so they volunteered unabashedly citing these reasons: patriotism, loyalty to the United States, peer pressure, boredom, adventure, and even to protect their families from FBI or other governmental agency pressures. The War Department thereby raised the Hawaii quota and 2,600 left Hawaii on the one time luxury liner *Lurline* on 4 April 1943.

In transit to Oakland with typical Hawaiian panache (the characteristic free spirited "Hawaiian style" of life,) "shooting craps" took over during their spare time and this very probably led to the regiment's motto, "Go For Broke" (Shoot the Works.)

With approximately 4,000 men, far larger than an ordinary infantry regiment the army organized them into the 442nd Regimental Combat Team—the three infantry battalions to be supported by the 522nd Field Artillery Battalion, 232nd Combat Engineer Company, Medical Detachment, 206th Army Ground Force Band, AntiTank Company, Cannon Company, and the Service Company.

The 442nd trained at Camp Shelby, Mississippi, from April 1943 and became a superb ready-for-combat unit. They had overcome their initial language, cultural differences and the jealousies which had cropped up between the

Hawaiian "Buddhaheads" and the mainland "kotonks." By 1 May 1944, they had departed from Virginia and zigzagging across the Atlantic they reached Italy in June 1944. The 100th joined the 442nd at Civitaveccia on 11 June 1944; it took the place of the lst Battalion which was left at Camp Shelby to train replacements for the 442nd.

Combat

The 442nd was attached to the 34th "Red Bull" Division and saw successive combat from Belvedere, Sasseta, Castellina, Colle Salvetti, Livorno, Pisa and the Arno River near Florence. The heroic Nisei soldiers lost heavily in 239 being killed, 17 missing, 972 wounded, and 44 injured in non-combat actions. But their greatest battle came in Northern France's Vosges Mountain campaign, 27 October-30 October 1944. They were desperately in need of rest and respite from combat, yet, they were ordered into battle by Major General John E. Dahlquist of the 36th Texas Division to rescue his "lost" lst Battalion, then surrounded by Germans.

His 2d and 3d Battalions were unable to break the siege. Despite suffering huge casualties, the 442nd displayed their spirit of "Go For Broke," and in a daring but murderous charge the 442nd broke through and rescued 211 men. The

442 in their courageous effort during the four days of nightmarish combat lost l61 KIA, 2,000 WIA, and 43 MIA—they had lost more men than those rescued. Companies I and K lost tragically. Company K had but 17 reporting for duty the following day and Company I had but 11 left for duty. The 442 was now down to one third of its normal strength.

After holding the "quiet" front in southern France, dubbed by wags among of the 442nd as the "Champaign Campaign," they were back in Italy by special request of General Mark Clark in March of 1945. Replacements had now joined the remaining veterans and the 442 was attached to the 92nd Division and soon broke through the tough Gothic Line and were into the Po River Valley when war ended in Italy on 2 May 1945.

Interestingly, when the 442nd was transferred back to Italy, its 522nd Field Artillery Battalion was detached from the combat team to support the assault into southern Germany. There they were the first US units to come across and liberate the Jewish holocaust camps in Dachau, Germany.

The Israeli government has recognized the liberating actions of the 522nd and have included a plaque picturing the 442nd patch logo in the Dachau death camp's museum.

Citations

The 100th Battalion/442nd RCT is recognized today as the most decorated unit in the US armed forces. It has 18,143 individual decorations for bravery and seven Presidential Unit Citations. At war's end the unit's final roll call listed 650 KIA, 3,536 WIA who were awarded the Purple Heart medal—some being cited twice or more times for wounds, 177 were injured in noncombat activities, and 67 were MIA. In recognition of its valorous deeds and record the 100th Battalion is still on the active rolls of the United States Army as an US Army Reserve Unit in Hawaii and its colors are often displayed in ceremonies and parades.

Legacy

The legacy of the Nisei soldier to the present generation of Nikkeis and indeed, to greater America, is legion. In Hawaii, the AJA veterans, supported by the GI Bill of Rights, quickly completed their higher education, then organized socially and politically into their 100th, 442nd, and MIS Clubs and by 1954, they led the Democratic Party and wrested control from the long intransigent Republican Party of Hawaii. They were able to elect two senators to represent Hawaii in Washington, both with 100th and 442 ties: Senators Spark Matsunaga and Daniel Inouye. Later in the 1980s George Ariyoshi, who served in the MIS, was elected governor of Hawaii. The distaff gender also sent congressional representatives from Hawaii, they being Patsy T. Mink, and Patsy Saiki.

On the mainland, not to be out done, California voters elected Senator S.I. Hayakawa, and Congressmen Robert Matsui and Norman Mineta; certainly a miraculous feat when viewed in the historical light and record of California and western states' outright racism and discrimination against the Isseis, Niseis and all AJAs and other Asian Americans.

The 1952 law that allowed alien Japanese to become American citizens by passing a citizenship test would not have been probable had not the Nisei soldiers sacrificed all, even their lives, to prove that AJAs were true Americans.

Statehood for Hawaii came in 1959 after long delays prior to the war because of the astounding record of Americanism shown by the Nisei soldier.

As many Issei proclaimed "we can walk with our heads held up high because our sons and daughters, the Nisei generation, fought for all of us."

Our standing in American society today, the acceptance of the present Nikkei generation into America's middle and social stream of life, and to some degree even our professional and economic livelihood, can be attributed to and traced to the courageous sacrifices of the World War II Nisei generation. We are truly indebted to the Nisei soldier for he has provided to the younger Nikkei the legacy that we enjoy today; dignity, respect, and often the admiration of America's greater majority.

The Hope

I hope that all who read this book will appreciate how far the Nikkei or Japanese Americans have come in Minnesota and America. I hope that the sons and daughters and the grandchildren will read these stories and biographies of our Minnesota Nikkei soldiers and appreciate the "Greatest Generation." It is particularly necessary here in Minnesota since so many are descendants of *hapa* (interracial) marriages. It is imperative that they know their proud and beautiful ethnic background and very important, the historical and cultural contexts which provided their presence and acceptance in today's Minnesota. I hope that this book will be the stepping stone for you, the progeny of the Niseis to ask questions, to dig deep and come to understand your Issei, Nisei and other Nikkei ancestors.

CHAPTER ONE

Toshio W. Abe

Toshio William Abe was born on 27 June 1919 at San Diego, California. His higher education included San Diego State College, University of California, Berkeley, University of California, Los Angeles, and the University of Minnesota where he received a mechanical engineering degree in 1947. [1] Tosh was drafted on 2 April 1941 by the US. Army at Ft. MacArthur, CA. and received his basic training with Company B, 7th Medical Battalion, 32nd Infantry Regiment, 7th Infantry Division. There he learned to administer to the wounded and his daily regimen included reveille, chow, police or the proverbial clean up of the company area, field medical training and the endless lectures on what is expected of a medical aid man and of a medical unit in combat. He looked forward to the weekend "passes" and anticipated the Christmas leave and after that discharge for draftees were to be in for one year. Then came Pearl Harbor and this affected and drastically changed his and everyone's lives—especially Americans of Japanese ancestry and the Issei, parents of the AJAs.

Incidents

Tosh remembers that the day after the December 7th attack all Fort Ord service personnel were dispersed and

dispatched to all corners of the reservation—no one was left in the cantonment area in order to minimize casualties from any enemy bombing and shelling. Then units were sent to guard

Toshio William Abe addressing the 1999 memorial for AJA deceased veterans at the Fort Snelling National Cemetery.

all coastal areas against hostile landings. Fortunately no landings occurred; incidentally, almost all Nisei troops were without arms and those few who had arms were without ammunition.

On a cold, wet, windy January day of l942 Tosh's unit was guarding an oil depot near Morro Bay, California. The most exciting event that occurred then was the torpedoing of an oil tanker by a Japanese submarine and the unit was ordered to and did rescue members of the tanker crew.

By March of 1942, according to Tosh, all AJA servicemen were informed, without any explanation, that they would be shipped "inland." Fort Leonard Wood, MO., Camp Hood, TX, Ft. Custer, MI., Camp Grant, IL., Ft. Sheridan, IL., Cp. Robinson, AR., Ft. Bliss, TX., Ft. Sam Houston, TX., Cp. Wolters, TX., Cp. Shelby, MS., Ft. McClellan, AL., an army camp near Cheyenne, WY., Ft. Jackson, SC became the new destinations for these hundreds of Nisei soldiers. There, they became the core of the DEML (Detached Enlisted Men's List)—euphemism for an army labor battalion. Tosh was sent to Camp Wolters, TX along with approximately a hundred others from Ft. Ord and about seventy five from Ft.

Camp Savage, Winter, 1942

Lewis, Washington. There they were detailed to cleaning up barracks littered by recruits passing through the camp, garbage and trash detail, latrine clean up, and the rock breaking detail that was usually reserved for the army stockade prisoners. It was difficult for Tosh to believe that Uncle Sam appreciated the true worth of AJA soldiers—was this to be their permanent war time service and contribution to the war effort? (2)

One morning in May 1942 DEML Nisei soldiers were called into formation and informed that orders had been cut for Tosh and nineteen others to entrain for Fort Snelling, MN. When they arrived at Headquarters Fort Snelling, no one knew anything about them, until someone recalled that he had heard that the Army was opening Camp Savage, a one time "old men's camp," that had also been a one time CCC (Civilian Conservation Camp). Tosh described Savage, slightly south of Minneapolis, in the following graphic words:

> The town of Savage looked just like it sounded; a gas station, a general store, a restaurant, and city hall—all ma n' pa operations,—dirt streets. Nearby was "Camp Savage" consisting of six log cabins (barracks,) a mess hall, and a latrine building, which also looked like log cabins. This "complex" was formerly home for aged

men, a place where the state dumped old men to live out their lives.

According to Tosh, this was transformed into the "New" Camp Savage, United States Military Intelligence School. The personnel consisted of the Commandant, staff of officers, a number of civilian language teachers who were Niseis and Kibeis. There was also a Headquarters Company, maintenance personnel, and finally the students who were predominantly Niseis and Kibeis (Niseis who were educated in Japan), with a handful of Caucasian military personnel.

Toshio Abe, next to Savage historical Marker.

He was in the first "cycle," it was scheduled for six months and he graduated in December of 1942. This was the initial graduating class from Camp Savage. Despite his eagerness to serve, it was not until January 1944 that Tosh received orders to leave Savage for overseas duty. He, it turned out, was a victim of Army, Navy bureaucratic suspicions and bungling. [3]

Combat in Burma

Tosh was soon on his way overseas—destination the China-Burma-India (CBI) Theater, landing at such storied places as Perth, Australia, Colombo, Ceylon (now Sri Lanka,) Calcutta and Delhi, India, Ledo, Myitkyna, Bhamo, Indaw, Burma (now Myanhmar.) Tosh's MOS (military occupational specialty) called for him to serve as an interpreter/translator, and he did so at SEATIC (Southeast Asia Translation and Interrogation Center in New Delhi) but the NCAC (Northern Combat Area Command) travails in northern Burma stand out. He, along with many of the Niseis sent to Burma, served valiantly as combat infantrymen, slogging through the wet, humid, tangled jungle and disease laden mountainous country.

Tosh was flown into newly captured Myitkyna in 1944 where he replaced the original Niseis in the 5307th Composite Unit (Provisional,) commonly known as "Merrill's Marauders." Myitkyna was the major supply point in Burma resupplying the Chinese fighting the Japanese in China. He was soon transferred to the "Mars Task Force" (US. 475th Combat Infantry Regiment) which was the unit relieving the 5307th then scheduled to rotate to the states. (4)

Toshio Abe interrogating wounded Japanese POW in Burma, 1944

The "Mars Task Force" was considered not quite combat ready and in need of more training so the much in demand Nisei linguists were assigned to the British 36th Division which was then battling the crack Imperial Japanese 18th Army Division, veterans of many South Pacific battles.

According to Tosh they were actively engaged in obtaining tactical and strategic intelligence through interrogation and document translations. Tactical intelligence vital to the success of a mission was often obtained by wiretapping

Japanese field wire lines and a few ultra brave and audacious Nisei infiltrated lines, eavesdropped on enemy conversations and barked out orders in Japanese leading to their capture or demise.

Tosh recalls vividly doing intelligence work in combat, carrying and firing his rifle or carbine, hurling hand grenades alongside the infantryman. He faced double jeopardy since he was fair game to the enemy and to unknowing itchy fingered American soldiers and so some Niseis on the front lines had personal "buddy" soldiers who stayed close to them with automatic guns. Commanders and combat soldiers acknowledged that the Nisei linguists with them on the lines were truly infantrymen and awarded them the coveted and well respected Combat Infantryman's Badge. Combat, in Burma, Tosh says, was particularly hellacious:

> The problems confronting both the Allies and the enemy were not only the confrontation with each other, but jungle diseases such as malaria, jungle rot, dysentery, bush typhus, blood suckers, along with combat fatigue (often referred to as psycho neurosis.) Many of the men succumbed to such diseases, were incapacitated and sent back to the rear echelon.

In describing low morale problems and terrible physical

ailments Tosh blames the "wet, wet, wet" weather and the prevailing jungle growth. They were major factors in lowering the effectiveness of the fighting force.

"The monsoon season," Tosh says, " begins in March and extends into September and this introduced us to conditions never experienced before. Our clothes were damp and moldy, twenty-four hours a day. If you had a leather billfold it disintegrated within a short period of time. Our GI leather combat boots had to be replaced by canvas, rubber soled jungle boots. One could not wear a wrist watch; the band, even if it were nylon, would cause a rash to develop on the wrist. Air Force leather jackets fell apart and had to be replaced by nylon jackets." Unit morale suffered even in the best of units such as "Merrill's Marauders," because the jungle, mountainous terrain, humidity, continued rains, diseases, ferocious combat and the long distances traversed kept the unit in Burma without fulfilling the longed for promised "rotation to the states."

Tosh was in continuous combat for eight months and was awarded the Asiatic Pacific Theater ribbon with two battle stars, the American theater ribbon, Good Conduct medal, the W.W.II Victory Medal and three overseas bars.

Tosh was finally relieved from his Burma combat duty in March 1945 and returned to the states for discharge in September 1945 via the Indian Ocean, the Red Sea, the Suez Canal, the Mediterranean, the Atlantic and New York, having spent 22 months overseas. Tosh was honorably discharged at Camp Grant, Illinois on 13 November 1945, having spent four years, seven months and eleven days in the United States Army.

Tosh and Mary Abe are the parents of three grown children, JoAnn Toy (2 sons,) Matthew (1 son, 1 daughter,) and Mark. Tosh, a mechanical engineer, has been retired from 3M Company since November 1990 but continues to do consulting work.

End Notes

[1] Tosh tried to obtain a delay of his induction since his father had died on 3 January 1941 and his mother was alone. His request was denied.

[2] This was certainly a low point in the career of Tosh in the US Army. He said, "the manner in which the Nisei soldier was treated and regarded by their Caucasian fellow soldiers is a disgrace and the armed service should not have condoned such a policy of harassment, intimidation and general verbal abuse."

[3] Tosh was held over from any shipping list for over one year despite his many requests to be sent overseas. His mail was being opened, and when the Adjutant was confronted he was informed that he was considered a high security

risk! Why; his father was a pioneer in the San Diego fishing industry, and Tosh was considered a possible enemy agent since he had taken a picture of the Oakland Bay Bridge under construction way back in 1937! *Naval Intelligence* at work! Fortunately, Tosh was able to convince the authorities that he was a loyal American soldier and Tosh was sent overseas in 1944.

[4]The 5307th Provisional Group was a volunteer group composed of veteran infantrymen. This unit had Nisei linguists who fought as infantrymen and slogged over 500 miles of Burma's toughest jungle terrain and its objective was to clear northern Burma of the Japanese who were threatening to cut and capture the supply roads leading into China.

CHAPTER TWO

Tom T. Oye

Tom Takeshi Oye was born on 22 October 1918, in Hillsdale, Oregon. He received his high school diploma from Salem High School, a B.A. degree from Willamette University and a Juris Doctor degree from DePaul University.

Tom was drafted into the U.S. Army on 20 February 1942 at Fort Lewis, Washington. Tom's early army experiences featured duty as a member of DEML (Detached Enlisted Men's List). Many Nisei soldiers were in the DEML since the Army would not place them in regular TO&E (Table of Organization and Equipment) units, especially those located on the west coast. DEML members were in reality, a labor and service unit and the Niseis were moved inland to places like Camp Crowder,

Tom T. Oye

MO, Fort Riley, KS, Camp Hood, TX, Fort Warren, WY, etc. Tom said,

> Many of the tasks were menial, boring, dirty—officer's orderly, guest house gardener, quartermaster mechanic, freight handler, kitchen police, etc. To the credit of these soldiers even the humiliation of being locked up in a quartermaster garage with machine guns pointed at the exits to prevent them from seeing President Roosevelt on a visit to Fort Riley (did not) stifle their zeal to be the U.S. Army's best. For example, Pfc Kazuo Masuda was frequently lauded for his work as the Camp Crowder Guest House gardener. Later, he was assigned as a cadreman to the 442nd and quickly rose to the rank of staff sergeant. Soon he was in combat and received the second highest decoration, the Distinguished Service Cross posthumously.

Tom indicated that there were many other cases where, despite the heart rending situations and worries of their parents and family members in concentration camps, the Nisei soldier valiantly fought on...the spirit of *Gambare* ruled!

Incidents In Combat

Tom was assigned as a replacement to Company B, 100th Infantry Battalion* and came under his baptism of fire in the Vosges Mountain battle to rescue the Texas "Lost Battalion." He served under DSC winner, Lt. Allan Ohata, and remembers vividly that cool October afternoon, 1944, when German bullets began to snip the overhead branches. Tom says,

The reality of war came into sudden focus, when the following morning as we pushed forward, a rifle grenade came whistling in. It's proximity led me to immediately conclude that I was about to become a casualty. The expected 'bang' did not happen and in its place there was a 'sizzle' like a hot poker being immersed in water. Luck was with me!

Two days later I saw for the first and last time an enemy soldier in a field of battle. We were in the middle of the effort to rescue the 'Lost Battalion' of the 36th Division. Our forward movement was dislodging the enemy from their position. On this afternoon as we moved forward an enemy officer jumped out of his foxhole and started to run to join his comrades in retreat. He was quickly felled by our gunfire.... His body shuddered with each shot...The trophy collectors quickly converged on him, removed his pistol, taken as a souvenir or trade booty item.

That night my foxhole was dug next to a dead enemy. When the objective was reached, Co. B was ordered to place themselves in a holding position.The fall rains came and filled our foxholes, soaking our feet and threatened the onset of trench feet.When dry socks and shoe packs finally arrived I felt greatly relieved only to find that rain soaked feet when warmed swell and become unbearably painful.

The "Riviera Campaign"

After the Vosges Mountain campaign Tom was assigned to Headquarters Company as the Communications Sergeant. This was the time of the oft remarked Riviera "Champagne Campaign," which was not without combat action and citations for bravery as the 442nd continued patrolling against the enemy. According to Tom, Company headquarters was in a beautiful mansion owned by an American financier. The Italian housekeeper, who had remained in the home became their cook. On New Year's eve, Tom says, "She dug up the champagne she had buried in the garden to save it from the Germans and we toasted in the new year (1945) and devoured the delicious pasta she prepared for us." Tom recalled, "I still have an unset opal she gave me when she learned of my October birthday." It had been brought from New Zealand by her seaman husband whose where abouts was not known at that time.

Gothic Line and the Po Valley Campaign

On 25 March 1945, the 442 (minus the 522nd Field Artillery Battalion) was reassigned to General Mark Clark's Fifth Army in Italy. The 442nd was attached to the IV Corps and placed under the control of the 92nd Infantry Division. It turned out to be the last campaign for the 442nd as the Germans surrendered in Italy by 2 May 1945. The Gothic Line was Germany's impregnable defensive bulwark and Clark had repeatedly thrust units against the line to overcome the Germans. All failures until he was able to commandeer his favorite, the 442nd. It was in the fading throes of this great war, Tom observed that,

• Pfc Sadao Munemori dove over a German hand grenade to save two comrades. Munemori was posthumously award-

43

ed the Congressional Medal of Honor.

• First Lieutenant (now U.S. Senator) Daniel K. Inouye's right arm was nearly blasted away by a German rifle grenade as he led his platoon in a fire fight against the enemy. Inouye received the Distinguished Service Cross. Tom remembers:

> Desperately digging a foxhole only to find a huge boulder two feet down. I dug around it but ended up sharing an uncomfortable shelter. To further aggravate the situation the hot Italian sun beat down on the rocky ridge
>
> My other memory of the campaign was as a member of Major Mitsuyoshi Fukuda's Task Force carrying the ammo can for the machine gunner, jumping crevices where a misstep invited disaster, sleeping on a rock ledge, fording a wide stream and walking on with wet feet …

Tom commented also about the humorous sight of seeing some of his combat buddies with cackling chickens and squealing little porkers packed away in their knapsacks for their next chicken fry or barbecue even as they marched and hiked to the next combat line.

Of all things that he missed the most, Tom said, "I missed

the permanency of a home and old friends...most of all my wife and child."

Post War

Tom became the Battalion Sergeant Major after combat under the direction of 100th Infantry Battalion Commander Lt. Col. Mitsuyoshi Fukuda. Tom was awarded the prized Combat Infantryman's Badge and the Bronze Star for Meritorious Service, the Mediterranean European Theater of Operations ribbon with three battle stars (North Appenines, Rhineland, and Po Valley campaigns.) He continued in the Army Reserve for an additional 25 years and retired as a Lieutenant Colonel.

Civilian Life

Tom's civilian background includes 35 years of credit management with 15 years of Board of Directors service, the National Food Manufacturers Credit Group; 20 years as Commissioner, Edina Human Rights/Relations Commission; 10 years member National Panel of Consumer Arbitration, senior member; member of the University of Minnesota President's Advisory Committee, Asian Pacific Americans.

Conclusion

Tom is the father of two adult children, Thomas Asa, and Audry and has one granddaughter, Emiko. Tom's spouse was Martha Inouye Oye (deceased 1996) In conclusion Tom writes:

> In the heat of war, one must wear humanity as a shield to ward off those forces that destroy those qualities that make us the species that we are. I came to the fuller understanding of the devastating effects of war—particularly on those whose lands are the battleground. I conclude with a statement of admiration and respect for those who pointed their course towards restoration of those rights denied peoples of Japanese blood; I applaud the focused vision of the Hawaiians that centered on statehood for their islands, an equitable share in the social, economic and political structure of their islands. To all who brought honor to the 100/442 a very solemn salute!

* The 100th Infantry Battalion, originally made up of draftees from Hawaii first entered combat at Salerno, Italy, in September 1943. Their unparalleled courage resulted in

tremendously high casualty figures; in their first five months of combat, the 100th went from 1,300 men to 531 able bodied men. Thus, their monicker of the "Purple Heart Battalion."

CHAPTER THREE

Dr. George T. Tani

Dr. George T. Tani, also known as "Tad" for Tadashi, was born on 16 December 1915 in Oakland, California. He grad-

uated from Oakland Technical High School, June 1932, and from the University of California School of Optometry, June 1939. In 1950, he graduated from the University of Minnesota Medical School and served his internship at Ancker Hospital in 1950-51. In 1955, he completed his Ophthalmology Residency at Rochester Mayo Clinic and in the same year, George entered private practice in Saint Paul. Along with his private practice, he was appointed to serve on the clinical teaching faculty at the University of Minnesota, Department of Opthalmology

Dr. George Tani

World War II Years and Military Service

At the outbreak of World War II in December 1941, George was working as an optometrist in Oakland, California. In 1942, George and the Tani family were detained at the Tanforan Race Track Assembly Center and then transferred to the Minidoka camp in Idaho, where he was assigned as the camp optometrist. After about six months, he received clearance for a job in Chicago. He had plans to apply for medical school or to join the army.

George entered the US Army on 4 October 1944, and was assigned while working in Chicago and after basic training he volunteered to go to MIS at Fort Snelling, Minnesota, graduating in the summer of 1945. He was in transit to the Pacific theater when the war ended.

Occupation Duties

George landed in the Philippines on 20 September 1945. He was stationed there for about a month before being assigned as translator/interpreter to the Chief Surgeon's Office AFPAC, Tokyo Japan. His duties with the Surgeon General's Office included accompanying Commander Gore to interview the General Staff of the Japanese Army, Navy, Air Force and the Medical Corps.

In November 1945, He was assigned to the US Typhus Commission in Tokyo. The mission of this commission was to prevent the outbreak of typhus throughout Japan. The method used was by using DDT to kill lice. Innoculations were given to those infected with typhus. He accompanied the field officer staff of the Typhus Commission as translator/interpreter. This assignment sent him to all ports of embarkation where repatriates were returning, as well as to many of the larger cities in Japan—Yokohama, Osaka, Hiroshima, Fukuoka, Nagasaki, Beppu. He returned to Tokyo to file reports, then on north to Sendai, Aomori and Hokkaido. He was also active in taking pictures of hospitals and patients in connection with the work. He investigated and reported on the epidemiology of typhus in Yamagata Prefecture. Among those he worked with were Colonel Sadusk, head of the unit; LTC Wheeler, second in command; and Major S.F. Blanton, entomologist.

After completing assignment with the Typhus Commission, George was assigned to the US Public Health and Welfare Department under General Sams making photographic documentaries on various aspects of health conditions in Occupied Japan such as:

- The Drug scene in Tokyo including the raids on drug peddlers and black marketers.
- The "Poor houses" which were temporary shelters of

those bombed or burned out of their homes.
•The malnourished children with bloated abdomens.
•The returning Japanese soldiers from overseas posts.

Impressions and Observations

When George arrived in Japan in October 1945, his immediate impressions were that Japan was a devastated and defeated country and that he wanted to help the people in need. Since his occupation duties required travel throughout Japan, he was able to observe first hand the total devastation of the war and the atomic bombings. Noted were:

- Devastation of Tokyo: not a building on the Ginza … blocks of rubble with a large steel safe on a concrete base. Destruction was total from Tokyo to Yokohama
- Hiroshima was gone with no buildings—ghost trees—no one there in November of 1945. The destruction of the Atom bomb (was total).
- Nagasaki was bombed but the homes behind the hills were intact.
- Kagoshima was devastated by a "system" of multiple bombing attacks. The planes would drop the remaining bombs on their way home to their base in Okinawa.

However, the railway stations and tracks were intact. Kyoto, Nara, Nikko, Ise were not touched with all their beautiful art and castles.

Sendai and Aomori in northern Honshu were bombed. People were starved, with many homeless. Mothers could not breast feed their children. The general public was on a starvation diet on the government ration plan. Malnourished children with bloated stomachs were a common sight.

Medals and Citations

George's medals and citations include the following: The USA Typhus Commission Medal for "meritorious service rendered in connection with the work of the USA Typhus Commission in control of typhus fever in Japan, November 1945 to 30 June 1946;" American Theater ribbon, Asiatic Pacific Theater ribbon, Victory Medal, Good Conduct Medal, Army of Occupation Japan Medal, two overseas service bars, and the Presidential Meritorious Unit Citation ribbon.

George's WWII rank was Technical Sergeant, and he was Honorably Discharged on 12 November, 1946. On 20 August, 1948, he completed the prescribed course at the Medical Corps ROTC training camp, Fort Sam Houston, Texas. On 10 June 1950, he was appointed First Lieutenant,

Medical Corps in the Army of the United States.

Medical Career

George's private practice became known as Tani Eye Associates in the seventies when both of his sons became ophthalmologists and joined the practice. He continued to be active on a part time basis. Along with his practice, he served for thirty years on the clinical faculty, Department of Opthalmology, University of Minnesota. He joined the faculty as Clinical Assistant Professor, and retired as a clinical Professor in 1986. His current status is Clinical Professor, Emeritus, Department of Ophthalmology, University of Minnesota, and he belongs to the following professional organizations: American Academy of Ophthalmology, Minnesota Academy of Ophthalmology, American College of Surgeons, Minnesota Medical Association, and Ramsey Medical Society.

Civilian Life

George's career was replete with contributions to the community and the nation. He served as president for the following organizations:

- Minnesota Medical School Alumni Society 1985-86
- Japan America Society of Minnesota 1989-90
- North Maplewood Lions Club 1994-95
- Past president and member, Mayo Clinic Ophthalmological Society
- He was a member of Doctors Mayo Society Church affiliation: Centennial United Methodist Church
- Alumni Service Award, Vision Foundation, U of M, 1991
- Asian Pacific Leadership Award for Community Services and Health Services, State of Minnesota, Council on Asian Pacific Minnesotans, 1993
- City of Saint Paul Mayor's Award for Community Service from Mayors Vavoulis and Latimer

George and Yoshi (Uchiyama) Tani were married in the Fort Snelling Chapel in1945. They have two sons, Paul and Douglas, (both medical doctors/ophthalmologists) and a daughter, Kay Tani (dance/movement therapist); and seven granddaughters.

*George died on 22 March 1999.

CHAPTER FOUR

Minoru (Min) Yoshida*

Min Yoshida

Min was born on 16 December 1918 in San Francisco, CA. He began studies at the University of California, Berkeley, but with the advent of war he and members of his family were moved inland to the Topaz Concentration Camp, Utah. He was able to continue his schooling at Dakota Weslyan University, Mitchell, S.D., where he received his B.A. degree in economics and history in1944. Soon however, Uncle Sam called him and he was sent to Camp Hood, Texas for basic training. He was then sent to Fort Snelling, Minnesota for his language training.

Occupation Duties and
First Impressions of Japan

Min arrived in Tokyo in the fall of l945 and after a short

stint at GHQ, Tokyo, he was assigned as a Technician 4th grade to the 9836 TSUCE (Technical Service Unit Corps of Engineers.) His duties included interpreting for his unit's officers, interviewing former Japanese engineer officers, and translating captured equipment, booklets, short manuals, and directions. As for his impressions Min remarked,

> Japan was a thoroughly defeated country. Destruction everywhere. The people seemed to be afraid, no, that's not the word, I guess they were more awed of us, the American soldier. They were certainly curious, and interested in us, the Nisei. We looked like them, yet we were in American uniforms. They were friendly and very curious about our parentage, background and how come we were in the American army.
>
> They were so short of food—I often brought them food, cookies, gum, chocolate candies that I purchased at the PX and gave them to our Japanese office staff. They were so appreciative and would say, *Arigato, Arigato, Arigato.*

Postwar and Civilian Life

Since his brother and family had already relocated in Minnesota Min and Mary also decided to stay in Minnesota.

Despite the cold winters Minnesota was an ideal place to raise a family and the fact that the kids enjoyed the neighborhood, schools, and social life, and most important, Min enjoyed his work; this made them become permanent Minnesotans. Min worked in finance at the Minneapolis Parks and Recreation Board for 31 years. He retired but continued to contribute his talents in many organizations. Prominent among his voluntary services have been: Treasurer of the Harron United Methodist Church; Camden Community News Board (20 years); and he and his wife Mary were volunteers at the ARC Value Village Store, New Hope, Minnesota.

Min and Mary are the parents of three adult children, Debbie Schwanke, Marlys Walters, and Mark Yoshida. They are also grandparents to seven grandchildren., and great grandparents to two great grandchildren.

* Unfortunately, Min succumbed to cancer on 17 May 1997.

CHAPTER FIVE

Harry Tsutomu Umeda

Harry Umeda's parents left Wakayama, Japan, in 1910 and emigrated to Sacramento, California, where they eventually settled on a farm. Two older brothers soon came from Japan and a third son was born in 1912. Harry, the fourth son, who was born in May 1915, remembers his early life:

> At home we spoke only Japanese. I did not speak a word of English until I started my first grade. This was [a] common situation amongst (the) population in our area. Except for one caucasian boy who was [the] son of [a] school janitor, the entire student body was composed of Japanese descent. We got along fine in [the] learning process. We were very diligent in our effort to learn the English language. We did not have very much contact with other racial groups until we entered secondary school.

Since the older boys and his father were busy on the farm from dawn to dusk, it was his mother who served as his mentor and adviser impressing and drilling into him the value traits of perseverance, being humble, polite, gracious, loyal, expressing gratitude, and observing filial piety. She constantly reminded us, "Never lie, it is a grave sin, and the *kamisama* will punish you, if you lie! *Bachi ga ataru!*"

Unfortunately, his mother died at the early age of 55, when Harry was but fourteen and so Harry went to live with his eldest brother and his wife. Harry remembers those days and his kindly sister in law: "My sister-in-law had three children and took care of me as if I were her son. She was exceptionally kind to me. I can still picture her darning my socks and washing my clothes on a wash board."

Harry's father always wanted to own his own farm but due to the California Alien Land laws of 1913 and 1920 Issei could not own land. It was a kindly and friendly caucasian couple, Mr. and Mrs. Landsborough, who helped with the formation of a farm corporation. Harry and his immediate older brother, both citizens, were to be the shareholders with Mr. Landsborough to be guardian until he and his brother came of age. When the state of California approved the corporation it was with great happiness that the Umedas came to purchase and own sixty six acres of land. The Umedas had become landowners—no longer were they share croppers and this pleased his father immensely for he had come to be a landowner in his own lifetime! "Father," according to Harry, "retired from farming and returned to Japan two years after the death of my mother. After the war, the American Red Cross informed us that my father had

Harry Tsutomu Umeda

died during the war."

Harry did not become a farmer, however. After graduation from high school he enrolled and graduated from Heald's Business College of Sacramento and looked forward to work in the business field but alas, the climate of the times was against Harry. Depression times, racial antipathy and with war clouds forming in Asia and Europe, he was unable to find employment.

Selective Service, The Draft, PreWar Service

After acrimonious debate the Selective Service Act was passed by Congress in September 1940—all males between the ages of 21 and 35 had to register—by the end of October 1940 the first draftees were inducted for twelve months of training. Harry's number was 20 and he was drafted into service on 3 February 1941 and he reported for basic training at Watsonville, California with the 250th Coast Artillery Battalion. His pay: $18.75 a month. Harry remembers his uniform as vintage World War I with puttees, park ranger type hats and OD colored woolen uniforms, brown shoes and boots.

After basic training the 250th CA Battalion was alerted to leave for Kiska, Aleutian Islands, Alaska. A few days prior to departure orders came down the pipeline to reassign all AJA (Americans of Japanese Ancestry) soldiers to other units since Kiska could be readily attacked by Japanese forces. About seventeen of us were transferred to the 17th Infantry, 7th Infantry Division., Ft. Ord, CA.

Wedding

Harry and his wife Ethel (Imagawa) were high school friends and as the war clouds gathered, and after "many many months of courtship," Harry says, they decided to marry. It was in Virginia City, Nevada, on 26 July 1941; Harry and Ethel suffered through a long distance marriage since she could not join Harry at Fort Ord. Ethel stayed home in Sacramento and Harry hurried home from Fort Ord on weekend passes. Rumor was rampant that married draftees would serve one year only but all that was rumor. Pearl Harbor changed everything for everyone.

Pearl Harbor

December 7,1941 was traumatic and particularly wrenching to Harry. Here's how Harry remembers that day.

> The morning of December 7, 1941, Pearl Harbor, Hawaii was attacked by Japanese forces. All weekend passes were cancelled. We were ordered to make wartime gear and be prepared to move farther away from Monterey Bay.
>
> That evening I found time to telephone Ethel. This was (a) very very sad parting—not knowing where we are going to be. We bid (a) sad but pleasant goodbye. I was calling from (a) public phone booth. As I hung up the receiver, I knelt on my knees and sobbed. This moment of terror has been deeply etched in my heart. It will never go away. Even today that terrible sobbing pain surfaces.

Post Pearl Harbor

Harry along with his unit were shipped out via Greyhound Bus from Fort Ord to Half Moon Bay, California. After several days Harry and all Nisei soldiers were moved to Santa Rosa for detached duty, really meaning doing nothing. Then it was on again to Gilroy where the Niseis were quartered in a large onion center warehouse which served as the assembly center for all Nisei soldiers awaiting reassignment further inland because of Executive Order 9066.

On 24 May 1942, according to Harry,

> After many days of traveling by train, first going east, then going west we finally reached our destination, Camp Savage, Minnesota, a onetime CCC camp, and later, a senior citizens home (camp.) We were the first Nisei soldiers assigned to Camp Savage.Everything was sparse, we had to sleep on the floor on a mattress and even studied Japanese on the floor. We had to clean up the living area and we 'made do.' We did bring the camp to comfort level right away. I remember George Kanegai as the first sergeant, the senior NCO of the camp, who was a good soldier—his jovial personality fit the Nisei soldiers who were under great stress at Camp Savage.

In the interim, Ethel joined her parents, younger sister and brother at Tule Lake Camp for two months until she received permission to come to the Twin Cities—this was

August 1942. She soon found employment helping to take care of a family and their children.

Combat Incidents In New Guinea

After graduation they were formed into nine men Translator and Interpreter Teams and left for Australia by air on 12 April 1943. They reached Brisbane on 15 August 1943 but had to undergo more waiting, training and in general, it was really four months of boredom. Then they were shipped out to New Guinea where they faced jungle living for the first time. According to Harry,

> We were smack in the middle of the jungle with combat all around us. We immediately dug deep two-men foxholes next to our operational and sleeping area tents and made them into secure bunkers with logs and large rocks, plus dirt and camouflage shoveled over to protect and disguise our foxholes. On our second night sirens wailed signalling an air raid by Japanese bombers. They attacked our position with many antipersonnel bombs and I had to cringe deeper into my foxhole. It was an awful scary experience with bombs falling all around us!

The next morning we examined the damages and I noted that saplings three to four inches in diameter were downed by the exploding shrapnel and the nearby jeep was riddled with shrapnel holes. Fortunately, no one was killed or wounded. As days and nights continued we were bombed often, true, some were nuisance raids and we became more accustomed to such air raids, but every raid meant increased trepidation and fear in me with the thought that one of those bombs may have my name on it.

Work of the Language Team

Our language team was located on the east central coast of New Guinea. This was the Central Japanese Prisoner of War Compound and Harry came face to face with the Japanese enemy as they were processed by their team in the compound. This is where, Harry says, he faced the realities of war:

As our combat troops brought the POWs in they were in a malnourished, starvation state—all were in extremely poor physical condition. Many were but skin and bones, weighing about 80 pounds. Some were delirious. Those injured or wounded had had little or no medical attention. They were carefully nourished and brought back to good health by our forces. The food and medical attention were deeply appreciated by the emaciated POWs. This aided greatly in our next step—the interrogation, We interrogated the prisoners for combat and strategic intelligence. These are highlights of my interrogation experiences:

• First, almost to a man the prisoners were astounded that they were being interrogated by a person who looked like them and had knowledge of their language, customs and cultural heritage. They had little if any knowledge of American Niseis.

• The fact that they had been treated humanely, having been fed, clothed, housed decently, and medically taken care of made them greatly appreciative. The fact that they never received any training in POW life and nuances made them answer all our questions truthfully...they literally "spilled their guts out."

• Interrogation, I found, is really experiential. Interrogation is not a method to be learned purely from the textbook. We did not learn interrogation techniques at Savage— we were trying, at that time, to master the difficult Japanese language.

• Every prisoner was different. One had to develop a variety of techniques, and to me this was the most interesting phase of interrogation.

• As the guard brought each prisoner to me he would stand at attention. After carefully examining the prisoner's papers, I would determine his physical condition; eyeballing him, I would then make up my mind concerning the approach to take: soft or hard. It depended also on the psychological state of the prisoner, the type of intelligence needed, and the immediate or later importance of the intelligence.

• The soft approach was pleasant: I would offer him a cigarette, gum,hard candy, chocolate, drink of water, etc. and begin plying him with questions of his home, family, school, prefecture, relatives, job, etc. Then gradually lead into the military questions, usually OB (Order of Battle, i.e., unit designation, chain of command, commander's names and ranks, adjoining unit designations, weaponry, objectives, etc.)

• The hard approach was generally unpleasant for me and there were times when I would switch with someone more adept at this approach. No pleasantries, no handouts, you would have the prisoner standing at attention all through the interrogation, you would scowl, use a gruff commanding voice and direct tone in all the inquiries. I've seen many a prisoner become so fearful, especially if you threatened to report their POW status to Tokyo headquarters and to their parents, that they lost control of their bladders and wet their pants, some even defecated. I understood the fear that war can bring to an individual for I, too, underwent the same experience during my first air raid. The hard approach was used mostly against hardened NCOs and officers—those suspected of lying or giving misleading information.

• All during the interrogations I kept thinking that these prisoners were my enemy and they were the ones that brought me into this jungle. But as one human being to another, such events brought sadness and tears to my eyes.

Combat In The Philippines: Leyte, Mindoro Islands

In October 1944, our team went by troop transport from New Guinea to the landings taking place at Leyte Gulf, Leyte Island, Philippines. Even as we disembarked in eighteen feet high waves, climbing down the nets to our bobbing landing boats, Harry witnessed the huge firepower of the US naval ships and dive bombers of our army air force. They lambasted Leyte's eastern shore line. This was late in October and the desperate Japanese navy initiated their Kamikaze attacks against the ships in Leyte Gulf from 25 October on so Harry was happy to be on land by this time. Most of the Japanese defenders on Leyte had withdrawn to the northern portion of the island and their major elements and leading officers had gone to the major island of Luzon.

According to Harry,

> We encountered a sergeant major who had been told to defend the area with his small contingent of troops—the officers had all left to go to Luzon for the final defense under General Tomoyuki Yamashita. The overwhelming firepower and numbers of American troops and weaponry in contrast to their starved, emaciated condition made it evident that they could not possibly defend

and win—so he surrendered!

Three weeks later, Harry and his buddies were on their way to combat in Mindoro island, adjacent to the large island of Luzon. A few weeks thereafter, Harry's Team Leader, Lt. Elmendorf came bearing beer and the best news out for him. After two years of overseas combat and living in the jungle Harry was awarded a sixty day furlough with transport home by air. Harry said, Lt. Elmendorf was a great team leader and everyone respected him. Harry's team members were:

Lt. Elmendorf, Berkeley, CA. (Team Leader)
Kim Hatashita, Terminal Island, CA.
Minoru Namba, Sacramento, CA.
Richard Hirata, Huntington Beach, CA.
Ralph Kimoto, Parlier, CA.
Kenneth Shimbo, Seattle, WA.
Hideo Tsuyuki, Los Angeles, CA.
Sam Umade, Fresno, CA.
Kaoru Nishida, Fresno, CA.
And one other

Furlough In Minnesota

Harry and Ethel spent some time visiting his brothers and

their families in the war relocation (concentration) camps in the various states and this was hard on the psyche of Harry—he couldn't fathom why they should be incarcerated and denied their freedoms.

The subtleties of discrimination were clearly evident to Harry when he and Ethel began their search for an apartment. The apartment advertised in the paper as being "for rent" would not be available as they inquired at the front door. The owner, upon seeing them would say, "Oh, I'm sorry, another party just rented that apartment this morning (afternoon.) Angry but what could Harry do?... and soon his sixty days came to an end.

Harry put in for an extension through Fort Snelling's MISLS commandant who put in a strong supporting statement for Harry. Colonel Kai E. Rasmussen, the commandant, had Harry visit all the ongoing MI classes to describe what duties of a linguist was like in the Pacific War. Soon Colonel Rasmussen notified him that he had been granted a sixty-day extension and he continued visiting classes and informing students what was in store for them in the field.

The sixty days ended and still no apartment, so Ethel decided to stay at her employer's home working as a domestic helper. Harry then reported to Camp McCoy, WI. to return to his unit. Harry was notified at Camp McCoy that he had enough points to be mustered out of the army. Happily, Harry remembered his mother's sage saying, "If there's a beginning there must be an end."

Discharge and Return to Minneapolis

So Harry T. Umeda, 39076153, Staff Sergeant, Headquarters, 24th Infantry Division, U.S. Army, was honorably discharged on 24 August 1945, at Camp McCoy, Wisconsin. He was awarded the following medals and ribbons:

- Asiatic Pacific Service Ribbon with two bronze stars
- Philippine Liberation Ribbon with two bronze stars
- American Defense Service Ribbon with medal
- Good Conduct Service ribbon and medal
- Three overseas service bars

Civilian Life and Family

Instead of returning to the west coast Ethel and Harry decided to make Minneapolis their home. Ethel found a job in the hospital field and he enrolled in a private accounting school under the GI Bill of Rights, After eighteen months of schooling, Harry was employed in a small hospital where he learned the "ropes" of hospital financing and management for four years.

Harry was happy to be in hospital work and continued to forge ahead. He became the comptroller of Northwestern Hospital for two years and when the Corporate Offices, Fairview Health System of Minneapolis offered him the post of Comptroller and Director of Finance he joined the system in January 1956 and remained there until his retirement in June, 1980.

Harry and Ethel* have been married almost fifty six years and they have one son, David and his wife, Linda, a grandson Corey (16) and one granddaughter, Angela (11).

* Unfortunately, Ethel died on 19 January, 1998.

CHAPTER SIX

Mitsuso Yoneji

Mitsuso (Mits) Yoneji was born in Nawiliwili, Kauai, Hawaii on 7 October 1920. He spent his earlier years in the islands and graduated from Kauai High School. After graduation from high school Mits decided to enroll at the University of Redlands, Redlands, California. It was here that he learned of the attack on Pearl Harbor, 7 December 1941.

Mitsuso (Mits) Yoneji

When Executive Order 9066 was declared by President Roosevelt Mits went to San Bernadino to enlist in the US Army on 24 February1942. He was driven to March Air Force Base, Riverside, CA. along with six caucasian volunteers. He said,

I was singled out and told to wait in another room by myself. I waited several hours until they told me that my papers were in order and I was then taken to Fort MacArthur, San Pedro, CA. The driver left me at the gate—they would not let me into the post. When eight pm arrived they "booted" me off the base so I hopped on an electric train which took me into Los Angeles. I secured a hotel room and slept soundly until the following day—I still wanted in!

The following morning Mits walked over to Los Angeles City Hall and signed up—this was the 25th of February l942. He was bused to Fort MacArthur where he took the physical exam, passed it and issued GI clothing. He had finally made it into the army!

Basic Training

Soon, thereafter, he was once more singled out to join a group of Nisei recruits—this was the first time he realized that other Nisei soldiers were in his vicinity—he was in a group of thirty. Mits said:

We were all trucked to L.A. depot and loaded on a sleeper with a black porter—this was my first train ride! We were on our way to Camp Robinson, Little Rock, Arkansas for our basic training. The train was a slow 'milk runner' stopping at almost every town and city on the way—it took us almost a week to get to Camp Robinson. We were fed either on the diner or in the by way towns and cities on the way—time hung heavy—I even recall having a swim at the Fort Worth, TX YMCA pool since we were hung up there for a long time.

Once at Robinson, ten Niseis were assigned to each of three companies and further subdivided one Nisei to each tent of five. His cadre sergeants were all from the south so Mits was very leery about the forthcoming training—he had heard and had premonitions about how southerners treated nonwhites. Training was hard and rough but his fears were unfounded as the cadre treated them judicially and seemed to be sympathetic and at times, openly pulling for them as underdogs. They even invited him to join them for dinner and a movie in Little Rock.

Incidents

After basic training the Nisei trainees were all ticketed to go to Minnesota to attend the Military Intelligence Service Language School at Camp Savage. During basic Mits had been bitten by a chigger and infection had set in. Mits refused to attend sick call fearing that he would be left behind. At Camp Crowder, MO. more Nisei soldiers joined them and entrained to go to Minnesota. At Springfield, MO. during an extended stop, having run out of cigarettes, Mits decided to hobble across the street, over a viaduct to purchase his cigarettes at a store. While on the viaduct Mits took a couple of camera shots of the tracks leading out of town.

As Mits stepped out of the store a policeman confronted him and took him to the police station. There he was questioned and locked up. The following morning he was offered bread and water for breakfast—he refused and so a police escort was formed to accompany him to breakfast in town.

When he got back, Camp Crowder's Intelligence Officer, a Colonel Steele was there awaiting Mits. Noting that he was hobbling, the colonel pulled up the pant leg and inspected his leg. Mits was immediately told that he will be checked into the camp hospital. As Colonel Steele and Mits were being driven the colonel stopped the car and he bought a newspaper.

On the front page the newspaper had featured Mits' picture with a big headline screaming "Jap Soldier Caught."

This was an embarrassment to Mits and he was relieved to be hospitalized, out of the public eye and questioning.

After the doctor lanced the infection he was soon on the recovery road. One day he was surprised as the nurses sympathetically urged and took him to the hot springs to soak and swim in the curative waters. Mits, having recently gained a pay raise from $21 to $50 a month as a private, gratefully accompanied them and after the outing treated the nurses to a shake at a nearby drug store. Mits was very appreciative to them for their show of kindness.

Return to Duty

Upon full recovery Mits was sent back to his barracks and he was duly surprised at the great number of Nisei soldiers who were now part of his unit, Headquarters Company, Camp Crowder, MO. They were, apparently, a holding company, where all Nisei soldiers were temporarily held prior to further assignment—many were sent to Camp Shelby and the others to MISLS, Camp Savage, Minnesota.

Mits noted that Tom Oye, as the company clerk and a Sergeant Wakamatsu were the only Niseis with stripes then. The rest were privates. There were over five hundred of us there, according to Mits.

It seemed that every time a new army camp was built or where they needed labor reinforcement, Niseis were the manpower. When we heard that Hawaii's 100th Infantry Battalion was in Wisconsin, another Hawaii soldier, Pvt. Shinichi Sakai and I went in to see the commander for a transfer to the 100th—our request was denied.

Then, in the spring of 1943 we heard that the army was seeking U.S. born Nisei soldiers to become cadre for the newly formed 442nd Infantry Regiment to be trained at Camp Shelby, Mississippi. We applied but once again we were turned down, this time by the 'dumb' first sergeant who speciously argued that Hawaii born Niseis are not native (US) born.

In the fall of 1943 Mits was finally able to get away from Camp Crowder when he and other Niseis were sent to Camp Savage to be trained as MI linguists. Mits was surprised when he met his older brother who had also volunteered from Hawaii, along with other Hawaii Niseis. Mits graduated in the spring of 1944 and fifteen of them were sent to Fort Monmouth, N.J. where they, along with twelve caucasian soldiers were formed into a signal intelligence unit.

While stationed in New Jersey, Mits, along with many of his buddies visited New York. New York has wonders and sights galore but it was the presence of his future wife, Toshiko Baba, that endeared New York to Mits. A courtship of six weeks ended with their marriage and Mits and Toshiko honeymooned at Niagara Falls and Minneapolis. As Mits remarked, "The army finally did me a good turn...a lifetime of blissful living."

Duty Overseas

During May 1945 Mits was sent overseas from Seattle to final destination Okinawa. Mits reflects that,

> We took about a six week's 'cruise' to the South Pacific, then on to Okinawa—the fierce battles had pretty much ended by the time we got there in July l945. I was in Okinawa when the war ended on 15 August 1945.

Soon thereafter, Mits and his unit were sent to Korea for occupation duty as interpreters. Mits worked as an interpreter in providing signal communication to US Army units in the Seoul area. On 1 January 1946, he was on a ship headed for Seattle. The army then flew him to New York City and Mits was discharged from Fort Dix, New Jersey on

1 February 1946.

Mits received the Asiatic Pacific Theater ribbon, Occupation (of Korea) ribbon, and the Good Conduct medal.

Civilian Life

Mits graduated from Drake University, Des Moines, IA with a Bachelor of Science degree in Pharmacy. Mits and Toshiko came to Minnesota in 1954 and he worked as a pharmacist in the Bloomington area retail drug stores.

Mits and Toshiko are the proud parents of three children, Sheryl and Carol (twins), Jerald, and 5 grandchildren.

CHAPTER SEVEN

Isamu (Sam) Sugimoto

Isamu (Sam) Sugimoto was born in Yuma, Arizona, on 10 December 1924. His parents ran a successful pool hall business until the depression and the coming of the war. He and his mother ran the business for nine years when his father became ill with tuberculosis and Sam remarked that he came to be a pretty good pool player, learning the ins and outs of the pool game.

When Pearl Harbor occurred Sam was a senior in high school and they (an older sister, Sam, and mom) were sent to Mayer, AZ. Assembly Center on 8 May 1942, but his father was kept in the County hospital in Yuma. Three days later his dad died and the family returned temporarily to Yuma for the funeral.

Isamu (Sam) Sugimoto

Sam Joins The Army

In June 1942, Sam was sent to the Poston Relocation (Concentration) Camp. When the call for volunteers for the 442nd RCT was announced he quickly volunteered but they rejected Sam; undaunted, Sam volunteered to join the Military Intelligence Service (MIS) at Camp Savage, Minnesota.

At Savage the Army tested his Japanese language ability, found it to be unacceptable and so he was assigned to Headquarters Company, School Battalion, Camp Savage, MN. There, he performed all the supernumerary tasks assigned to casuals (gofor, clean up, set up class rooms, office work, yard work, K.P., latrine orderly, fire guard—kept the barracks stoves piping hot, etc.,—all that good stuff as Sam put it.) Sam soon decided that he could do more for the war effort and put in for a transfer to the 442nd. The transfer finally came in April 1944—he had been at Savage since November 1943. Sam was sent to Camp Blanding, FL. for 16 weeks of combat infantry training. Then he was assigned back to Camp Shelby, MS. for a month as he was destined to become a replacement in the 442nd fighting in Europe.

Combat With The 442nd In France and Italy

Sam was sent overseas as a replacement in the 442nd RCT and he said:

> Fortunately, I missed the terrific "Lost Battalion" battle fought in the Vosges Mountains where the 442 lost more men then they rescued. They needed replacements badly. I was sent as a replacement to the Wire Section, Headquarters Company, 3d Battalion. I told the First Sergeant, "Sarge, I'm not a commo man—I was put in the HQ Company Communications Platoon, back in Shelby, by mistake—I was with them for only one month—I really was trained as a rifleman." He looked at me and must have thought I was a "nutcake"—he told me to stay in commo for the time being because we're short there. I was a "quick learn on the job" and in retrospect, the fact that I was not a rifleman may have saved me from being on the casualty list.
>
> We were then sent to Southern France where some enjoyed pleasant duties and some even termed it the "Champaign Campaign." For me it was my baptism to combat—this is where I came under fire for the first time—it

was scary and definitely not pleasant. Our sergeant was wounded and some of the rifle companies had significant casualties (KIA, WIA and POWs).

The 442 was holding a line along the French Riviera coast and into the foothills of Italy, they said, to block any German thrust from Italy into France during the Battle of the Bulge 16 December 1944 until mid February 1945. With the collapse of the huge German offensive in the Bulge Battle, we thought that combat was finally over for the 442nd but that was not to be.

General Mark Clark, Fifth Army Commander in Italy, was anxious to have the 442nd back into Italy. The German Gustav Line in Northern Italy was holding up progress in the Fifth Army's attempt to wipe out the Germans in the north, especially the fertile Po River Valley. So by early April '45 we were slogging up the mountains to turn the flank and secure the German Gustav Line. After heavy fighting and many casualties* the 442 cracked the Gustav Line and soon the Germans surrendered.

By 5 May 1945, the Germans had surrendered all of Italy and the 442nd was placed on occupation duty. Those who were replacements like me were to be the occupation soldiers since we did not have enough points to be sent home. I pulled eight months of occupation duty.

Campaigns, Awards and Decorations

Sam was awarded and decorated with the Combat Infantrymen's Badge, The Presidential Unit Citation, The Bronze Star, and the European Theater of Operations (ETO) ribbon with three stars (Rhineland, North Appenines, and Po Valley Campaigns. He earned other ribbons and medals such as the Good Conduct Medal, the Victory medal, the Occupation (Europe) ribbon, and two overseas bars. He was discharged honorably as a Staff Sergeant.

Civilian Life

Sam returned to school under the GI Bill and became a dental technician. His first job took him to New York City. There he married his wife Shizuko (Rose) whom he had met in the Poston, AZ. Relocation Camp earlier. They moved to Long Island, NY in 1948. They were blessed with three children, two daughters and a son.

In 1965 they moved to Minnesota. Judy, the eldest daughter is a nurse at the University of Minnesota, (3 children,) Ted is a surgeon doing missionary work in Zaire, Africa, (3 children,) and Edith, their youngest child is a veterinarian at Long Prairie, MN (2 children.) Sam is now retired and lives in Little Canada, Minnesota.

* It was during the final push in northern Italy that Pfc. Sadao Munemori was killed when he smothered a German hand grenade with his body, thereby saving his fellow soldiers. For this heroic sacrifice Munemori was awarded the Congressional Medal of Honor posthumously, then the only CMH given to the most decorated regimental sized unit in the US Army. It was during this final campaign that Lieutenant Daniel Inouye, now U.S. senator from Hawaii, lost his right arm when a German rifle grenade struck his right elbow.

CHAPTER EIGHT

Hisashi (Butch) Kumagai

Hisashi (Butch) Kumagai was born in Sacramento, CA on

22 October 1918. He attended the Sacramento Area High School in Clarkburg, CA. Soon after Pearl Harbor he and his family were removed to the Walerga Assembly Center and thence to Tule Lake Relocation Camp in northern California—this was in May of 1942.

Hisashi (Butch) Kumagai

In May 1943 Butch came to the Minneapolis area when a camp bulletin listed a defense training school in Shakopee, MN. Butch was soon disappointed when the school did not materialize—the host company had discontinued operations. Since jobs and schooling were readily available in the Twin Cities, Butch decided to stay and enrolled at Dunwoody Institute where he took up welding.

Butch Joins The Army and Sees Combat

Uncle Sam stepped in at this point and drafted Butch in June 1944 at Fort Snelling. He was sent to Camp Shelby, MS to be trained as an infantryman. By January 1945 he was overseas and joined the 442nd RCT as a replacement—this was in Marseilles and Nice, France.

According to Butch, "I just missed the heavy fighting that the 442nd was in at the Vosges Mountain rescue operation of the Texas Lost Battalion...I was indeed lucky!" He became a member of Company G, 2nd Battalion, 442nd Regimental Combat Team. He was in the 4th Platoon, as an ammo bearer for the 60mm mortar section. His first operation was easy in contrast to what was to come for the 442nd was relocated away from the Vosges Mountain area and was assigned defensive patrolling near the French-Italian border. This came to be known as the "Champaign Campaign" among the weary 442 combat veterans.

Memorable Incident

Butch recalls vividly his most memorable combat incident:

It was during the tough Appenines campaign fighting our way through Florence, Castelpoggio, and the Avila S. Teronzo region when we came to a flat open field area that we needed to cross to continue our advance to the Po Valley. The Germans had ample time to zero in on the field with their 88s.* It seemed like every yard was pinpointed as a target. We lost many brave men there and they were yelling for the medics. We didn't have enough litter bearers so our mortar section had to help.

We had to charge into the open, four of us on one litter to help rescue the wounded 442 men. "Man, the shells kept exploding all around us and I thought this was it! My number was gonna be on one of the exploding 88 shells. Hell, I was scared as hell! I'm sure some of us even wet our pants. But we had to keep going for our Nisei buddies needed to be rescued—we had to run like hell for one hundred yards or more to rescue all the wounded —we rescued every wounded man there. That was the scariest moment of my combat experience.

Butch ended up in northern Italy and they were busy processing German prisoners when the war ended there on 5 May 1945. Soon thereafter, he served in the Occupation

Forces in the Livorno area. Not having enough points, Butch served as a sergeant in the occupation until he was finally sent back to the states in August 1946. He was discharged from Fort Sheridan, IL. in August 1946.

Campaigns, Medals and Awards

Butch was awarded the coveted Combat Infantrymen's Badge, the Bronze Star, Presidential Unit Citation, European Theater of Operation ribbon with two battle stars, the Good Conduct Medal, the Victory Medal, the Occupation (Europe) ribbon, and two overseas bars.

Civilian Life and Family

Butch came home, got married to Terry Ogasawara in September 1946 in Minneapolis. Butch continued in his occupation as a welder in the Waterman Waterbury Furnace Company and finally retired in June 1985. Butch and Terry are the proud parents of two children, Gloria and Alex. and equally proud grandparents of three grandchildren, Mariko, Leilani, and Josh.

* The German 88mm gun was the most effective, accurate

and feared weapon according to all Americans who came under its fire. It was used as an antipersonnel, antitank and antiaircraft gun.

CHAPTER NINE

Edwin M. (Bud) Nakasone

Edwin Masanobu Nakasone was born in Wahiawa, Hawaii, on 29 April 1927. He was truly a "pineapple kid" having been born in a plantation cottage operated by the California Packing Corporation, (Del Monte Logo,) Camp

Edwin M. (Bud) Nakasone

No. 9, Poamoho, Wahiawa. He came from a large family of ten children, five girls and five boys—he being the fifth child.

He was, early on, intimately familiar with the local Japanese community for Wahiawa, then, ethnically, plurality wise, was Japanese. He attended kindergarten at Wahiawa Gakuen. In fact, there were three Japanese language schools in the community. He spent the next six years going through Wahiawa Elementary School and remembers nostalgically his Monday through Saturday daily schedule. From 8 a.m. to 2:30 p.m. it was the English Public School and from 3:30 p.m. to 4:30 p.m. he went to Wahiawa Nihongo Gakuen sponsored by the Hongwanji Buddhist Church. By 5 p.m. he needed to be home to prepare the ofuro (Japanese style bath) and "woe to me," he recalls, "if the ofuro was not ready for my father—he was always the first to take the ofuro bath." On Saturdays from 8 a.m. to 10 a.m. he had two hours of Japanese class time. In writing of these early days in Hawaii Bud reflects,

> Like many Niseis, the cultural regimen, formal Japanese classes, the ethnic celebrations, the Japanese spoken by the parents, relatives and neighbors—all these served to prepare me for the formal military schooling I received at the Military Intelligence Service Language School, Fort Snelling, Minnesota.

Pearl Harbor and WWII (Hawaii) Reflections

Bud remembers the Pearl Harbor attack as though it occurred yesterday for he was an eyewitness. He recalls getting up early that morning with the thought that he was going to join his friends at Nakamura (Shell brand) gas station. This is what Bud remembers:

> December 7th was a Sunday and the rest of the family were still sleeping so I got myself a bowl of cereal—Kellogg's Corn Flakes. As I sat munching corn flakes, I gazed westward out the kitchen screen door and I remember noting a group of planes swooping down, coming from Kole Kole Pass towards the large US Army post of Schofield Barracks. Then the planes, about a dozen of them, having strafed the post, climbed systematically, follow-the-leader style and dove down, one after another towards Wheeler Army Air Field. Then, I saw pellet like objects dropping to the planes that were lined up beautifully on the field. Instantaneously, I saw the exploding bombs—planes being blown up, hangars and buildings all destroyed and burning. I remember saying to myself, "Oh my God, the navy is making a horrible mistake,

they're bombing Wheeler Airfield." We were accustomed to seeing army-navy war games in Hawaii and I figured it was another one of these maneuvers.

Then, one of the zero fighters came zooming over our home—I dashed out just in time to see the plane and the pilot in it, no more than 250 feet above me and, sure enough, I noted the two red "meatballs" (the red sun of the Japanese flag) under each wing, and the meatballs on the fuselage of the plane. The cockpit of the plane was open and the pilot had his goggles on and his white scarf was streaming in the wind. I then realized that Japan was attacking us and that this was war!

I ran into the house yelling, "get up! get up! the Japanese are bombing Wheeler Field!" Turning on the radio I heard the announcer, Webley Edwards of radio station KGMB, blare out, "All servicemen return to your bases, all servicemen return to your bases— the Japanese are attacking Hawaii—Hawaii is under attack! This is no joke—the real McCoy!" This is how I remember the attack on Pearl Harbor.

Awaiting Army Induction

The war continued—1941 through August 1945. Nakasone saw and continued to remember the huge numbers of soldiers, sailors, and marines who came to Hawaii—many to train there for the Pacific campaigns. He recalls the government's call for Hawaii's AJAs (Niseis) to volunteer for the 442nd Regimental Combat Team. Over 10,000 responded in Hawaii and many of Bud's older relatives, friends and upper classmen responded to the call. Then in 1944 and 1945, it appeared that he was attending memorial services at the Hongwanji temple almost every Sunday for many of the local boys who were killed in action.

As the war ebbed farther away from the shores of Hawaii he wondered often if he'd be drafted since he would become eighteen in 1945. He kept hearing and reading stories of the boys in Minnesota—how they were studying hard and yet enjoying the friendliness and hospitality of the Minnesotans. He'd like that.

Induction and Subsequent Travels

Bud was in the August draft (1945) a few days before the end of the war—it was a large draft considering the small population of Hawaii at that time, close to 500 young men who, mostly, were recent high school graduates. Bud continues:

> We were trucked into Schofield Barracks from my town of Wahiawa, brought into Schofield's "Tent City," which was a huge induction area made up of five-man tents. I recall going through the regular administrative rigamarole, filling and signing all kinds of personal data forms. Then, one day, they called out all those with Japanese names, they lined us up and marched us into a building. Three Fort Snelling Nisei sergeants, greeted us and individually, asked us in Japanese, to read from a simple Tokuhon (Japanese language reader) that was mostly hiragana with a few simple kanjis—I'd say, about the second or third grade level, of our Japanese language schools. Those that passed, and I'd say almost all the Niseis passed, were ordered to go into an adjoining room—we were Snelling bound!

After a rough trip (he says he was not meant to be a sailor) via Army Troop transport, over 300 of the August Nisei draftees landed at San Francisco and ferried over to Angel's Island in the bay. Incidentally, he recalls vividly, the more garrulous local boys of Hawaii displaying their "go for broke" spirit in shooting craps—hundreds of dollar bills changed hands throughout the five-day trip. This was the first of five troop transport trips that he made during his army career. He remembers passing under the famous Golden Gate Bridge on 2 September 1945, the day that the Japanese surrendered on the battleship Missouri in Tokyo Bay.

They were transferred to Camp Beale, near Marysville, CA, but after a short stay there they entrained for Fort McClellan, Alabama, where the Hawaii contingent went through thirteen weeks of basic training.

It was Christmas Day, 1945, that they finally made it to Fort Snelling; they were assigned "quarters" in MISLS' Company E, the four-man, tarred paper hutments, which was popularly known as the "Turkey Farm." He recalled with pain, the unbelievably cold weather that Minnesota offered the sun loving Hawaiian Niseis. In fact, on his first pass out to Minneapolis, he mistakenly got off the trolley at Seven Corners, near the University of Minnesota's present day West Campus, and walked in ten below weather all the way to Hennepin Avenue. By the time he reached Hennepin Avenue's Kin Chu restaurant he was thoroughly frozen. To this day whenever below zero weather approaches he recalls that bone chilling, painful experience.

Duties and Studies at Fort Snelling

Since the next MISLS class was scheduled for March, l946, they were temporarily assigned as supernumerary troops (casuals) doing all the post's cleanup or "gofor" duties. In March, classes began and Bud remembers being in Section 14, there being 22 sections, with the more advanced students in the lower numbered sections. Classes were from 0730 to 1630, Mondays to Fridays; and on Tuesday and Thursday evenings all students were marched to the academic buildings for two hours of compulsory studies. Saturday mornings were devoted to inspections, parades and ceremonies. The curriculum concentrated on Japanese per se, with history and cultural elements sprinkled in, but heigo (military Japanese) was no longer taught and more civil administration (governmental) terms appeared through stenciled handouts.

By the end of June 1946, Bud's class, the last to begin studies at Snelling, was alerted to transfer the whole school to Presidio of Monterey, California. After almost four days of cross-country troop-train travel, they reached Presidio of Monterey and began classes there in late July. The presidio was in a picturesque location with charming towns and sites such as Monterey, Carmel, Asilomar, Pebble Beach, Fourteen Mile Drive, Fort Ord, etc. By December 1946, Bud had graduated and he remembers having made progress, advancing from Group 14 to Group 11. The class (those from Hawaii) was then shipped to Hawaii via Army Transport (he got seasick again) for two weeks of furlough.

Duty In Occupied Japan

In January, 1947, Bud arrived in Yokohama via army troop transport after eleven days of sailing—seasick again. He remembers his first impressions of Japan, the land of his ancestors thusly:

> It was cold and a blustery wind whistled into port. As I looked down on the dock I saw the Japanese laborers with threadbare clothing, with their olive drab military caps and black splittoed sandal like shoes and puttees wrapped around their legs—no gloves, no winter coats and they all looked cold. As some of the GIs flicked their spent cigarettes down to the dock the laborers scrambled to pick them up, snuff out the light and save them for future smoking or trading.
>
> Further signs of their defeat came to light when we arrived in the 4th Replacement Depot at Camp Zama, outside Tokyo. Crowds of young and old were at the barbed

wire fences next to the mess hall, where we lined up to wash out our mess kits. They were hungry and emaciated and the kids had red, frostbitten hands, and on their faces were frozen hanabata (runny nose—"snot"). All extended their cold hands through the fence line and were begging, "chocoletto, chocoletto, tabako, tabako kudasai!" (Chocolette, chocolette, tobacco please!) They all looked extremely hungry.

It was then that I reflected that Japan was truly a defeated land. Everywhere I gazed I saw burned out relics of brick and concrete buildings, factories that had been bombed and gutted out—no windows, just bare walls still standing like bereft, defeated soldiers— many with tall, grey concrete chimneys and the floors still lined with burned and abandoned, mute lathe machinery.

After about a week at Zama they entrained for ATIS (Allied Translator and Interpreter Section) headquarters, located at the NYK (Nippon Yusen Kaisha) building. There they were evaluated on their Japanese and a few were assigned to ATIS—the rest of them were later sent to Military Government (MG) teams of the various prefectures, line outfits, Counterintelligence Corps (CIC) units, Civil Censorship Detachments, Technical Intelligence units,

Repatriation work, military tribunal work, etc. There seemed to be a huge plethora of linguist requests from the various occupation units and the Nisei soldiers were assigned out to the units as required.

Awaiting their assignments, the linguists continued Japanese language classes in the NYK building and spent their free time in downtown Tokyo—a fabulous way to learn Japanese and become part of the native environment and culture. These were memorable days and many of the soldiers came to learn the meaning of the Japanese aphorism, "*shikata ga nai*," (It can't be helped).

Occupied Japan Remembrances

Bud was subsequently assigned to the 168th Language Detachment, Headquarters, 1st Cavalry Division, located in Asaka, Saitama Ken, a fast train ride thirty minutes north from Ikebukuro station, Tokyo. He remembers:

> • Allied occupation personnel were privileged—every train included a coach that had a wide white stripe painted on the outside with the words ALLIED PERSONNEL ONLY on it. Japanese were not allowed on the coach and they crowded themselves in the other coaches while the Occupation

coach was usually sparsely filled.

• The *tamanegi* (onion) existence held forth for Tokyoites—they were malnourished and starved. Often I saw men in old army uniforms and women in raggedy old mompei (women's wartime unattractive baggy slacks) cramped in the coaches, returning from a bargaining foray into the country. They had taken their treasured kimonos and were bartering them for rice and vegetables. As they peeled off their kimonos for food, tears were shed—thus the allegory tamanegi life.

• These poor individuals were often caught in a police net set up at the train stations and they had to empty all their precious gains from their knapsacks. Their government had a ceiling for each individual concerning rice and other vegetables and all amounts above that low ceiling were confiscated. Copious tears flowed then.

• A buddy of mine was invited by a poor family to have dinner with them. He accepted and noted that noodles was heavy on the menu but when he realized that his plate included the only egg for the entire family he graciously gave the egg to the children—soon thereafter he returned with a hand-bag full of C-rations, much to the appreciativeness and joy of the hungry family.

• On Saturday evenings, ATIS personnel flocked to the dances sponsored by the American Red Cross and American Recreational Services Personnel (akin to the USO stateside.) I noted that the Japanese young ladies, attired in formal kimonos, were especially in attendance. They liked the "dansu pahtay" since Nisei soldiers would willingly converse and socialize with them. Many Niseis made lasting friendships, and marriages ensued for some.

• During this difficult period the Japanese, in general, came to observe that America was a nation of expansiveness, sympathetic to the poor and defeated, kindly, nevertheless all powerful. Many remarked to me that their warlords were infinitely stupid to make war against America. I heard this sentiment many times, "You Nisei are a shining example of the greatness of America. You are Japanese in body, blood ties, and understand our culture; yet you are American in spirit and thinking and your great country has even allowed you to become a soldier in your honored army. You must help us by serving as the bridge of understanding between America and Japan. We must follow the leadership of America and become a democratic country."

Occupation duties, for Bud, were nondescript, routine, and generally boring. Everyday, interpreting for headquarters officers and NCOs. Interest heightened when he accompanied MPs on anti-blackmarket raids or while serving as interpreter for election observers in the local towns and communities. But nothing ultra-exciting happened, and as he neared the end of his eighteen months of army duty extension, (he had to enlist in the Regular Army in November 1946 in order to complete his MISLS schooling, graduate and serve in Japan) he gave serious thought to return home, go to college under auspices of the GI Bill, and receive an education to prepare for his future.

Army Reserve Duty 1948-1987

Bud was finally discharged from the U. S. Army on 17 July 1948, as a Technical Sergeant (today's Sergeant First Class) and he immediately enrolled at the University of

Hawaii, simultaneously signing up as a ROTC (Reserve Officer's Training Corps) cadet since veterans could become officers, second lieutenants, in two year's time. He recalls that his monthly cadet pay was $29. He graduated in June 1950 as an infantry officer from ROTC and was awarded his gold bars. Bud remained very active in the Army Reserves serving as the Commandant of the Fifth Army Area Intelligence School and was finally retired as a Military Intelligence Colonel on 29 April 1987, having served continuously for 41 years 8 months and 19 days. Bud was awarded the Legion of Merit, Meritorious Service Medal with one oak leaf cluster, Army Commendation Medal, WWII Victory Medal, Occupation of Japan Medal, Good Conduct Medal, Humanitarian Service Medal, Army Reserve Medal with three hour glasses, and the Army Reserve Achievement Medal.

Life In Minnesota

Though born and raised in Hawaii, Bud has spent the better part of his adult life in Minnesota. He is a University of Minnesota graduate and continued to teach history and international relations at Century College, White Bear Lake, Minnesota, until his retirement in 2000. Even after retirement, he has continued teaching history to young sailors, aboard ship through special arrangements with the U.S. Navy. He and Mary, a native Saint Paulite, are the parents of two sons, John and Paul. John and Jacqueline have a son (Jacob) and two daughters (Mariko and Natalie.) Paul and Susan are parents of a daughter (Sarah) and a recently born son, (Daniel.)

CHAPTER TEN

Isamu (Sam) Shimada

Isamu (Sam) Shimada was born in Woodbridge, CA on 4 March 1919. He received his primary education at the Houston Grammar School, and graduated from Lodi High School in 1934. Sam, along with his older brother then became farm custom workers where they specialized in all phases of tractor jobs, plowing, seeding, planting, cultivation, etc. They did this type of work until 27 October 1941, when Sam answered his country's call to the army. He was inducted at Sacramento, CA and he remembers receiving a "whole silver dollar to pay for his supper." He was sent by train to Presidio of Monterey where he was issued uniforms and by 30 October 1941 he was in Camp Roberts—East Garrison, CA to begin basic training.

Sam's "Ol' Camp Grounds"

Looking at the record Sam appeared to be the most travelled army man as he was shunted from one camp to another. It began the day after Pearl Harbor (8 December 1941) when all Nisei trainees were called out and ordered to turn in their rifles and their basic training was summarily terminated. On the 10th they were sent to Fort Lewis, WA for noncombat duty. He and the other Niseis were placed in the Detached Enlisted Men's List (DEML). Daily duties included the "mop and broom brigade"—they were to work on all the post's theaters, latrines, offices, and other areas needing cleanup services.

In March 1942 Sam was sent to Fort Snelling to drive trucks—he was informed that his knowledge of Japanese was too limited and he would not qualify as a student at the Military Intelligence Service Language School. The days at Snelling turned out to be a "good deal" when he opted to become a "permanent KP" with defined hours of work. This "good deal" came to an end when he was sent to Fort McClellan, Alabama, to train as a possible replacement for the embattled 442nd RCT. Dame Fortune smiled on Sam when he and

Isamu (Sam) Shimada

six other Nisei soldiers, for medical reasons, were not sent overseas to Italy as replacements. Instead Sam was sent to Fort McCain, MS; again it was detail work, clean up the post, range work. Sam was reasonably happy here for he was within travelling distance to Rohwer, Arkansas, where his mother and sister had been interned.

Sam recalls being issued a pass to visit his mother and sister at the Rohwer Camp. Hard luck dogged him this time when his bus broke down and this delay meant that Sam had but one day to visit before he had to return to Camp.

By July 1944 Sam was sent to Camp Forrest, TN where the army assigned him as a cook in the US Army prisoners stockade—a prison for "hard core" army recalcitrants. Sam treated all of them in his usual friendly and personable style and got along well with the prisoners. Soon thereafter he was sent to cook for the German POWs located in the same camp of Camp Forrest and even assisted the camp hospital's dietitian. There again, Sam relates, by treating the prisoners with kindness and courtesy his work brought "good results and it was very pleasant duty." The fact that Sam was a fast learner and having had two years of high school German meant that he was soon bantering understandable German to the POWs and they liked and appreciated his work and efforts to make life tolerable for them. As for Sam, he says "… as a Pfc, I was just trying to get by."

Sam's Civilian Life

The prison officers wanted him to stay on but the point system in effect then meant that he had 180 points. This was December 1945 and he was now at Fort McPherson, Georgia where he was soon discharged. His mother and two sisters came to live in the home that he had purchased in Minneapolis in July 1945 and so, he joined his family in Minneapolis. Sam has been self employed in Minneapolis as a distributor for the Alpine Indoor Air Purifier Company and the Japan Life America Corporation specializing in sleeping systems.

CHAPTER ELEVEN

Isamu Saito

Isamu Saito was born on 27 April, 1925 in Seattle, Washington. His family consisted of his parents and one brother. After going through the primary grades, he enrolled at Broadway High School but with the advent of war and Executive Order 9066 he and his family were moved into the Puyallup Assembly Center and subsequently transported to Camp Minidoka, Idaho. Like many Niseis Isamu received Japanese language training at home and at a local Japanese language school.

Isamu Saito

Camp Minidoka was located in southern Idaho, near the town of Twin Falls. The camp was crescent shaped and housed approximately 12,000 people. It was difficult to get adjusted to this environment. There was adequate food and housing; however, educational opportunities were very bleak. Eventually, despite teacher shortages and the lack of good educational materials, a camp school was established. A positive side of this unhappy situation was that new friends were made and at this age, all seemed like a holiday. The negative side was the fact of the tremendous sacrifices made by the older folks, parents and grand parents. They left behind all that was familiar and dear to them.

Army Training

On Isamu's 18th birthday, 27 April 1943, he received the notice from the government at Camp Minidoka. He had been placed in the enlisted reserve until he reached his 19th birthday when he received orders to report to Fort Douglas, Utah for induction and subsequent infantry training at Camp Shelby, MS. He was scheduled to go overseas with the 442nd Regimental Combat Team but due to illness Isamu was left behind at Shelby.

Based on his knowledge of the Japanese language Isamu qualified to go to the Military Intelligence Service Language School then operating at Camp Savage, MN, arriving there in August 1944, just in time to help move all equipment, supplies, books and other pertinent materials to Fort Snelling, MN.

Isamu was then assigned to Company H, MISLS as a student for the intensive nine months course in the language to include heigo (military Japanese language.) Schooling was very difficult, yet, he was able to graduate in May 1945 and was soon on his way to Camp Stoneman, CA, in the bay area where he boarded a troop transport, destination Manila, Philippines. He recalled it to be a long trip—they even had to stop temporarily in Hawaii for some refrigeration repairs but by June 1945 they reached Manila. Isamu recalls,

> Since the combat phase of the Philippines campaign was practically over, we practiced our conversational Japanese by interviewing Japanese civilians. The main topic was Japan as they remembered and knew it. We were priming ourselves, I suppose, to the coming invasion of Kyushu which was ticketed to be on 1 November 1945. It was an eye opening experience ... easy duty.

Duty In Occupied Japan

With the end of the war on 15 August 1945 he was transported by air and flew into Tokyo in October 1945. There, he was assigned as an interpreter with his principal duty at Ueno Station. The Third Military Railway Service served as the supervisory element over Japan's National Railway Service that provided railway transportation throughout Japan. Isamu in recalling his early impressions of Tokyo and Japan, said,

All Japan, especially Tokyo, was simply a devastated country—scenes of destruction, burnings, poverty all over. One couldn't imagine at this point, how the people could recover from such wreckage. There were hundreds of homeless, raggedly clothed people, some wearing wartime *mompeis* and leg wraparounds; all shivering in Tokyo's cold. These were daily scenes seen at Ueno Station. Many children, many adults, and many vagrants were all over the station seeking food, warmth and shelter; all seeking help and friendship. In spite of all this, I marvelled at their "*gambare*" spirit, never losing hope and exhibiting the Japanese trait of "*shikataganai*" even as we inquired as to how Japan began and lost the war—they accepted their conditions and tended to blame the military-industrial-complex for their losses and miserable state.

Isamu spent his off duty hours in Tokyo and in a "hideout" spa south of Yokohama getting there by rail. Extensive sightseeing was done during his furlough periods in beautiful Nikko, historic Kyoto, and the large bustling city of Osaka. Isamu was also able to meet his relatives south of Tokyo in Ito, and he was able to help them some by providing gifts of food, cigarettes, clothing, and other civilian consumer goods.

Discharge and Return To Civilian Life

By August 1946 Isamu's discharge date came up and so he was sent to Camp McCoy, WI where he was honorably discharged from the United States Army. Isamu was awarded the Asiatic Pacific Theater ribbon, Occupation of Japan ribbon, Good Conduct Medal and an overseas bar.

Since his parents and rest of the family were now in Minneapolis, he rejoined them there. He met his wife Judie in a Minneapolis Nisei Fellowship Group and they were married on ll August l951.

Isamu enrolled at Dunwoody Institute specializing in auto mechanics and graduated in June1953. Thereupon Isamu was employed at Quality Lincoln Mercury of Minneapolis. Isamu and Judie* are parents to Lorraine, Mark, and Elaine and have two grandchildren, Danielle and Joseph.

Isamu is now retired and works part time in custodial and maintenance work at the Southeast Christian Church in Minneapolis.

* Unfortunately Judie died of cancer on 4 March, 1998.

117

CHAPTER TWELVE

Toke Yonekawa

Toke Yonekawa was born on 10 October 1920 in Guadalupe, a truck farming region of California. He was the third child in a family of four boys and one girl. Toke attended elementary school in Guadalupe and Japanese school for two hours a day after his elementary school hours. He graduated from Santa Maria High School in 1939 where he earned three football varsity letters and two more in track.

With the advent of Pearl Harbor Toke and his family were evacuated to Tulare Race Track on 28 April 1942, where he worked as an orderly in the hospital until they were moved to the Gila River Relocation Center, Arizona. While at Gila River Toke worked as an ambulance driver and there he met his future wife, Tae Monden. In May of 1943, Toke was able to relocate to Detroit Lakes, MN, where he worked at a summer resort, and in September of that year, Toke moved to Minneapolis where he found employment as a cook at the Radisson Hotel. Toke and Tae were married in April of 1944 and one month later Toke volunteered into the United States Army, where he was soon assigned to the Military Intelligence Service Language School, Fort Snelling, Minnesota.

Toke's Military Career

After hard study at Fort Snelling, Toke graduated in May of 1945 and he was then sent to Fort Mc Clellan, Alabama, for a short stint of basic training. After basic training Toke was immediately sent to the Philippines where he was soon put to work interpreting, interrogating and translating at the Santo Tomas Camp of Manila. This was in the last period of the Philippines Liberation campaign. With the cessation of hostilities Toke was chosen to become a part of the first American troopers to enter Japan, landing at Atsugi airport on 25 August 1945. For Toke this was a memorable moment in his war experiences because as he got off the plane he distinctly remembers seeing all the kamikaze pilots lined up next to their planes, ready to take off to defend Japan, and many would have had the authorities not drained the gas tanks of each plane. Toke also remembers approaching some of the pilots and offering these dedicated warriors cigarettes. This surprised the pilots for they never envisioned an enlisted man, a sergeant and a Nisei at that, to display kindness and understanding.

Toke was attached to General MacArthur's headquarters located in the famed Dai Ichi building. He was soon promoted to Technician Third Grade—T/3 (this WWII rank is the equivalent, pay gradewise, to Staff Sergeant) and his daily duties centered around the translating of newspaper articles about MacArthur, the occupation and subjects concerning the U.S.Army. Another of his responsibilities included driving a Major Tilton, a University of Pennsylvania professor who lectured all over Japan. Toke's duty was to translate these lectures to the local populace. Toke remembers speaking about democracy in Tokyo,

Toke Yonekawa

Osaka, and Yokohama. In Hiroshima he remembers translating a particularly memorable speech about women's suffrage amongst the rubble created as a result of the atomic bomb. The room that the lecture was given in was the remains of a warehouse with a tin roof and no standing walls.

Memorable Incident

For one of the more memorable incidents Toke recalled the time he went to visit family and relations in the Mie Ken region of Japan. The village was near the Sea of Japan and many of the villagers collected salt and also grew rice to survive. While visiting Toke was asked if he would like to take a bath in the local bath house since it was his family's day to bathe. (In Japan, immediately after the war, due to the scarcity of fuel to heat the bath water constantly, each family was assigned a certain time and day to bathe at the local bath house.) When Toke and his immediate family arrived most of the villagers were already in the bathhouse to watch them bathe—word had spread that a visiting American would bathe at that time. When Toke voiced his great surprise, one of his cousins responded, "Don't worry, they're all family."

Toke's military service background includes the Philippines Liberation medal and ribbon, Asiatic Pacific Theater ribbon, World War II Victory medal and ribbon, Occupation of Japan medal and ribbon, and Good Conduct medal.

Toke's Return To Civilian Life

In August of 1946, Toke returned to Minnesota and attended Concordia College, where he also worked as a chef. While at Concordia, Toke helped to start and coach the Concordia Academy high school football, basketball, and he also began the track program at the college.

Then Toke began his own restaurant called *Toke and Pella's* which stayed in business for ten years. He then went to work as the chef at a popular restaurant in Saint Paul called the *Criterion* and he continued there for the next twenty five years. Toke is now retired and living in Roseville, Minnesota.

Toke and Tae are the proud parents of four grown children, Wayne, a National Institute of Health psychopharmocologist in Washington D.C.; Patricia, a University of North Dakota graduate and current manager of business properties; Mark, who lives in Saint Paul is in fiber optics communication work; and Paul, who lives in Steam Boat Springs, Colorado, is an owner and operator of a chimney sweep corporation. Toke and Tae are also blessed with six grandchildren with two of them about to become medical doctors.

CHAPTER THIRTEEN

Akira Fujioka

Akira Fujioka was born on 20 May 1930 in Stockton, California, the youngest of four children. His father owned a small printing shop specializing in Japanese and Chinese print jobs. The depression years were extremely difficult in

Akira Fujioka

generating a good living and so his dad sent his mom and the four children to Japan in 1933 when he was 3 years old. They lived with their grandparents and relatives in Okayama, Japan. In the meantime his dad stayed in Stockton keeping up the business and sending funds back to them in Japan. When the Sino Japanese War began in 1937, the monetary situation worsened as Mr. Fujioka lost his Chinese accounts. With the bombing of Pearl Harbor it was an almost impossible situation for the Fujiokas since their father was in the United States and the rest of the family was in Japan. Soon, they lost all contact as war continued until August 1945.

The War Years

Akira, as a young lad with US citizenship, faced some difficulties during his stay in Japan. When he graduated from primary school in Okayama City, the authorities did not permit him to enroll in their chugakko (junior and senior high school) because he was not a registered Japanese citizen—in fact, he was technically classified as an enemy alien!

So, his mother moved all of them to Himeji City, to start life anew hiding their connection to the United States. Himeji was bombed twice during their stay. There he and his sisters were enrolled in the chugakko and Akira graduated in 1948. When World War II ended in August 1945, they began a search for their father through the U.S. Consular Service in Kobe. Akira was finally able to locate his dad in 1948, who, during the war years, was placed in one of the concentration camps. His dad had relocated to Chicago after the war and so Akira decided to join his father, work and earn money to bring back the other members of the family to the United States.

Akira found employment doing assembly work in a Chicago furniture company and attended the Englewood Evening High School to improve his English. Two years later he graduated with a high school diploma. Akira had thoughts of continuing on to a college education, but Uncle Sam had other ideas.

The Korean War

The Korean War had started in June 1950 and more bodies were needed; Akira was drafted into the U.S. Army. On the 11th of September Akira reported to Fort Sheridan, Illinois, processed to Fort Jackson, South Carolina, where he completed sixteen weeks of basic infantry training and by March 1952, he was in Korea, having landed in Pusan. As an infantryman he went through Taegu and was assigned to be a replacement in the 27th Infantry Regiment, 25th Infantry Division, right on the 38th parallel area. This is Akira's observations:

> As I went up the peninsula of South Korea I noted the utter destruction—no vegetation in the form of trees, shrubs, and cultivated farms on the hillsides. Bomb, mortar, and shell craters abounded. The enlisted driver, having reached the base of the hill, said, "this is as far as I go, I don't want my head blown off—go up the hill and report in." With our individual weapons and back packs, two of us replacements struggled uphill and signed in.

Here Akira wryly remarked, "we didn't have any reception party. We were right on the 38th parallel and yet, because negotiations were going on, first at Kaesong, then at Panmunjong, we did not have any major offensive or defensive actions. At times, to me, it was almost a noncombat zone atmosphere during daylight, except for occasional incoming mortar rounds and patrol actions. However, these rounds did cause some casualties and it reminded me that we were at war. I kept thinking, I hope my luck holds out and particularly at nights we were always on alert."

Patrol Action—Akira Becomes A Casualty

Akira relates the following:

> We spent a good portion of our time solidifying our combat bunkers; the one on the line facing the enemy and the living bunkers which were on the back side of the ridge away from the enemy, where we slept and rested when off the line. My first impression of life as a combat infantryman was scary— I,we, all were fearful that we would be wounded or killed in this place. It was especially fearful when mortar rounds would occasionally come raining down on us and the bunkers. We became quite adept at hugging the ground in the trenches and bunkers when the firing started, especially during the

evening darkness. I didn't mind the rugged Korean terrain and night duties as much as others did, for it seemed that my earlier familiarity with Japanese terrain and night experiences of World War II with all its concomitant smells, dark silhouettes, and noises allowed my native instincts to sense and assess the environment better than others.

By this time Akira had been promoted to a corporal. He said, "No big thing—in fact, I was the lowest ranking noncommissioned officer and so I was called often to lead patrols to probe the North Korean lines." He became a casualty on just such a patrol. Akira explains:

It happened one night in August 1952. A tall, young, inexperienced lieutenant decided to gain experience by leading a patrol. In doing so, the lieutenant went ahead too fast without pausing to look around or listen carefully. I noted this and hurried forward to slow the officer's pace when the North Koreans sprung an ambush on us. The lieutenant went down, dead from a rifle outburst and I got hit in several places; later, I learned that a bullet went through my neck and hit a corner of my spinal column, another bullet smashed through my right arm above the elbow. A couple more bullets were stopped by my bullet proof vest. Two others in our patrol were killed and three of us were wounded, they informed me later. Fortunately for us we had followed the standing operating procedure (SOP) of having a backup patrol a few hundred yards behind us and when the North Koreans stepped out from their prepared ambush positions, our backup patrol wiped them out. The firefights lasted no more than five minutes.

Stretcher bearers were hurriedly brought in and soon I was airborne via a helicopter—my whole body was numb, and I had the distinct sensation as though I was floating. I spent two days in the field hospital, then I was transferred to Tokyo General Hospital where I spent two months with my right arm in a cast and my left arm and left leg were motionless due to the injury on my spinal cord.

Recuperation

Essentially, I was fully incapacitated. I was placed in the recovery ward since I needed 24-hour external help. After two months at Tokyo General Hospital the army sent me to Conus (Continental United States) in a military version of the DC6 after a two day stopover at Tripler General Hospital in Honolulu, Hawaii. They then sent me to Percy Jones General Hospital in Battle Creek, Michigan, for three months, and when that hospital closed, they sent me to Fitzsimmons General Hospital in Denver, Colorado, for six to seven months more of recuperation. I was finally discharged, medically, on 31 December 1953. My right arm motion was back almost to normal and my left side became sufficiently healed to support my weight and for walking. All movements gradually improved, although certain movements, such as my left arm and leg give me some trouble.

Decorations

Akira was awarded the Purple Heart, the Combat Infantrymen's Badge, the Korean Service medal with two battle stars, the United Nations Service medal, the Good Conduct medal and other service ribbons.

Post war Civilian Life.

Still, Akira needed to have the rest of the family brought back from Japan and reunited. Upon his discharge Akira worked at the Conrad Hilton Hotel in Chicago. As greater numbers of Japanese businessmen came to Chicago, Hilton needed someone fluent in Japanese to assist them and Akira's Japanese language ability came into good use. Since Roosevelt College was close by, he enrolled there, and thanks to the GI Bill and hard study, he graduated with a BA degree in Accounting in 1958. For a while he was employed in a small public accounting firm but soon he had the opportunity to go with the International Division of 3M, here in Minnesota.

In 1960, Sumitomo3M was incorporated and Akira became a key player in making this company operational. He literally commuted to Tokyo and worked there the whole year of 1962 and also in 1964. With 3M becoming more and more a global company Akira, with his bilingual and start-up expertise, was soon travelling on 3M business to Hong Kong, Taiwan, Manila, Malaysia, Singapore, Indonesia and Thailand. Akira is now enjoying his retirement with his wife and they have two children, a son and a daughter.

Epilogue

This is the remarkable story of one man's travails. A life of hardship during the depression years in two countries, America and Japan. He experienced life under fire from American bombing attacks during World War II as well as discrimination from Japanese authorities during the war. He returned to an unfamiliar America, his birthright, and soon thereafter he was placed as an infantryman on the Korean peninsula. Akira fought bravely for his birth country, suffered terribly from grievous wounds, and yet was able to succeed through education and hard work—he was imbued with the spirit of *gambare* (the spirit of persistence, of never giving up.) Akira had been tossed around by events beyond his control but he put his dual background to good use and became another shining example of our Nisei's courageous contributions to the United States in time of war and peace. His regret is that the Korean peninsula is still divided and can explode once again.

CHAPTER FOURTEEN

Paul Shimizu

Paul Shimizu was born on 24 April 1920, in Parlier, California. Paul came from a large family, seven boys and three girls, he, being the sixth in the family. His father was

Paul Shimuzu

a fruit farmer, concentrating on peaches and grapes at Clovis, California, which is close to Fresno. There, he went to elementary and high school graduating first from Garfield Elementary School and then in 1938, Clovis High School. Paul, then spent two years studying prepharmacy at Fresno State University when he decided to move to Oakland to matriculate at the California Chiropractic College. Paul graduated after Pearl Harbor and passed his California State Board Examinations in 1942, thereby becoming a doctor of chiropractic.

His dream of practicing in California was quashed with the coming of war and Uncle Sam had other ideas for Paul. Paul was turned down by the navy and the army air corps—

he volunteered but was denied serving for either services. The services were denying entry to all those of Japanese ancestry after December 7, 1941. Yet, Uncle Sam drafted Paul on 22 February 1942 at Presidio of San Francisco, California and he was next sent to Presidio of Monterey. Seemingly, the right hand of Uncle Sam did not know what the left hand was doing for Paul remembers succinctly, a close friend, Bob Goto, who was already in the army was discharged on 20 February 1942, as an undesirable citizen. From Monterey, Paul was sent to Camp Roberts, California, where he was in the Special Services Company doing menial chores, such as KP.

Then Paul was sent to Camp Robinson, Arkansas, for his basic training —this was the spring of 1942. After basic, Paul was sent to Fort Riley, Kansas, where he was in a Quartermaster company of the Fort Riley Cavalry Replacement Training Center driving trucks. His duty; delivering hay to the cavalry stables twice a day. Fort Riley was probably the last army post to have cavalry training and cavalry horses. Paul was stationed here until the spring of 1943. Then the call came for Nisei volunteers to join a combat infantry regiment to be composed of Japanese Americans—without any hesitation and feeling the need to do more as a soldier, Paul volunteered. This was in March 1943.

Paul Reports To Camp Shelby, Mississippi

As Camp Shelby was then being rapidly built up for combat training, Paul remembers the ubiquitous hurriedly constructed wooden barracks and "tent cities" so reminiscent of WWII training camps. He was soon assigned as a cadreman noncommisioned officer—this was approximately two months before the large contingent (over 2,500 men) came to Shelby from Hawaii. Paul and others of the 442nd cadre were busy constructing furniture (desks, shelving, benches, counters, chairs, etc. from packing crates and lumber scrounged from the camp supply dumps.

How Company

Paul was assigned as a supply sergeant to H Company, 2d Battalion, 442nd Regimental Combat Team. He remembers his commanding officer as 1st Lieutenant Christopher Keegan, the first caucasian officer that Paul came into close, direct contact. Lt. Keegan was a grand, fair, gentleman officer, who later retired as a regular army colonel and has attended the many H Company and 442nd reunions. Paul remarked, "I think he had a special feeling for his Nisei boys and we correspondingly looked upon him as our 'ol man." "H" or "How" Company was the Heavy Weapons

Company for the 2nd Battalion and we were equipped, along with our individual .30 calibre M1 or carbine rifles, the heavy water cooled .30 calibre machine guns, and the 81 millimeter mortars. "Damn, they were heavy to lift and lug but they sure did the job in providing close-in fire support for the front line infantrymen," Paul remarked. We worked hard at Shelby, the Hawaii boys and mainland boys, both in basic and advanced training and soon learned to become a united, smooth combat team. After training and maneuvers were finished we shipped out and by May 1944 we were in Italy.

Paul Experiences Combat

In May 1944, Paul was in Civiteveccia where he and How Company, along with the rest of the 442 came under fire. Paul said,

> Yes, I was scared as heck especially when we came under our first shelling. Shrapnel, rifle fire were coming at us and I heard the "zing, zing, zing" in our vicinity. I never dug so fast with my individual shovels as I did then. The German 88s were terrifying. This was especially so when they took advantage of forested areas as they introduced air

bursts which would cause death dealing tree splinters and shrapnel. This was especially so when we went into the Vosges Mountain area to rescue the Texas Lost Battalion later in October 1944. In this our initial battle we lost a lieutenant who was killed by German rifle fire, and two other men were casualties.

Then, Paul recited the litany of combat engagements he went through. Paul experienced all the major engagements of the 442nd. Livorno, Florence (for about three weeks,) the east side of the Italian peninsula, being shuttled back and forth to help other units, then to the Arno River area for three to four weeks. Then to Naples and we were shipped thence to Marseilles, France. This was in October 1944

From there Paul and the 442nd were transported by trucks, over 400 miles to northern France. Here, the 442nd was to engage in the bloody Vosges Mountain campaign. They fought gallantly to save the Texas "Lost Battalion"— the lst Battalion, 141st Infantry Regiment, 36th Infantry Division. The 2d and 3d Battalions of the Regiment had tried to rescue their lst Battalion brothers and had failed. So the 36th Division commander, Major General Dahlquist ordered the 442d to attack the entrenched German units who had surrounded the lst Battalion. "We've got to save them," he pleaded, and so the weary 442nd, after capturing and freeing the French towns of Biffontaine and Bruyeres, had to go back into battle. This proved to be the bloodiest campaign for the 442nd.

The Germans used their deadly accurate 88's to fire timed fire over the advancing 442nd. The tree bursts showered the brave Nisei infantry with death and casualty dealing shrapnel and tree trunks and jagged pine splinters. With the spirit of "*gambare*," (never say die, persevere against all odds) the 442nd even reverted to a so-called "*Banzai*" charge and finally rescued 211 members of the lost battalion. The price was unbelievable; in order to save 211 Texans, the 442nd lost over 800 men as casualties. According to Paul, "Rifle units were practically down to nothing—some companies were down to 15 men out of a normal complement of over 200 men." The battles took place in freezing cold and many suffered trench foot and other winter maladies. The campaign finally ended on 30 October 1944.

It was then that the 442nd was sent to southern France, where some dubbed it the "Champaign Campaign." Paul indicates otherwise, saying "We were in the vicinity of Sospel, France, and we continued patrol combat duty that did produce some casualties. It was really a time to reinforce the 442nd with replacements. By late March 1945, the 442nd, minus their artillery support, the 522nd Artillery Battalion (they were sent to support the American forces advance into southern Germany,) were shipped back to

Italy, via Naples. General Mark Clark, commander of the US Fifth Army, requested their return to Italy for the final push against the Gothic Line north of Rome and south of the Po Valley in northern Italy.

The Final Campaigns

Having returned to Italy, Paul remembers the hard fighting around Pisa, Carara (south of Genoa); at Carara they aided the 92nd Infantry Division capture a hill and Paul really felt the need of their accurate 522nd Artillery Battalion here—a lot of times the 92nd Division's artillery was firing into or too close to the 442nd's lines. They then captured Cunio, the little town where Mussolini and his mistress, Clara Petacci, were captured and hung.

At La Spezia Paul said,

> Germans were firing 12" artillery guns at us. One errant shell landed in front of us, 50 feet or so and it burrowed itself under the ground and came up on to the surface 100 feet behind us—it turned out to be a dud and did not explode. This was the closest call for me. Of all the artillery guns, I feared the German 88mm gun the most. It was the most accurate and had the highest velocity. One

would hear the "brrp" and that's all—no time to duck or hit the ground—it was at the target already.

My first day in combat in Italy was quite an experience. As we rode up to the combat area, I saw all the dead bodies. As the company supply sergeant, it was my duty to take the dead to the Graves Registration Unit. It was a very sad duty to see fellow Niseis dead and some were horribly mangled. But there were more German bodies than American and it was a macabre sight to see the Italian civilians burn up the German fatalities in order to prevent any epidemics.

Combat and Death

Having gone through heavy combat from the very beginning to the end, Paul was asked his combat feelings, thought, and general philosophy. He said:

I was scared as can be all the time. Soon, however, I developed a fatalistic feeling, I came not to think or dwell about it. I said and reminded myself, if you gonna get it, you're gonna get it. In combat, I did what I had to do and kept hoping for the best. I was careful as can be because we had mines all over and they did disable many of the front line troops. In some cases, the older soldiers developed combat fatigue—they tended to do too much thinking. The younger ones, with the spirit of "gung ho" or "go for broke" were the best combat fighters. I feel very fortunate, and surely was, as they say, "lucky as can be" to come back whole from all the 442nd campaigns.

Paul's combat duty ended at Milano. Then, he was sent to Naples for POW work. It was at Milano that war ended in Italy. It was "a great feeling of relief," Paul said. He was able to take classes at the University of Florence, in an Armed Forces program.

Honors and Decorations

Paul received many ribbons and medals for his long time service in the army but the more significant ones included the coveted combat infantryman's badge (CIB), the European and Mediterranean Theater of Operations medal, and the Bronze Star with a citation.

Discharge and Civilian Life

Paul, had enough discharge points, and was returned to the United States just in time for Thanksgiving, 1945. He disembarked at Newport News, Virginia , and was sent to Camp Beale, California, via air from LaGuardia Field, New York—he received his honorable discharge at Camp Beale—this was in December 1945.

Having returned to civilian life, Paul did postgraduate work at the Northwestern Chiropractic College which has since become the Northwestern College of Chiropractic located in Bloomington, Minnesota. He then worked for a chiropractic clinic for two years, 1947-1949. In 1949, he began his own practice in Minneapolis, and served his patients until he retired in 1997. Today, Paul and his wife Helene are proud retired parents and grandparents and continue to enjoy a full life of travels, visitations, and happy family life and reunions. Their three children (two sons and a daughter) have blessed them with five grandchildren (three granddaughters and two grandsons.)

CHAPTER FIFTEEN

Osamu Sam Honda

Sam was born on 24 January 1927, in Fresno, California, and was the third child in the Honda family, three boys and a sister. His father was a farmer raising all kinds of vegetables (carrots, beans, beets, cucumbers, tomatoes, etc.) to be sold at the Farmers Market and he also sold to wholesalers at contract prices.

Sam's Moves

Sam went to the Fresno Colony Elementary School and attended Washington Union High School for two years before war began. Then, Sam and family were all herded into the Fresno Assembly Center in March of 1942. The assembly center was in the Fresno County Fair Grounds and Sam remembers it as being "in the middle of the race tracks, no shade, hot as blazes, little wind, in meager, temporary black tarpaper barracks which had been hurriedly put up."

In September 1942, they were moved to the camp in Jerome, Arkansas, and Sam continued his schooling there receiving his diploma from Denson High School, Jerome, the War Relocation Authority operated school, in June

1944.

Having answered "yes, yes" to questions 27 and 28 of the WRA questionnaire, and desiring employment and freedom, Sam left camp and went to Cleveland, Ohio. There he found employment at Ryerson Steel Warehouse working as a laborer, moving steel rods about in the yard for the munificent wage of .65 cents and hour. He was then a young 17 years of age. At age 18 Sam was promoted to become a bridge crane operator beginning work at 0600 hours in the morning at a higher rate of .90 cents an hour—in the evenings he was taking classes at the Cleveland Trade School from 6 to 9 p.m.

Sam's Army Career

It certainly was a relief from his busy, busy civilian schedule when Uncle Sam drafted him on 23 July 1945. He was sent to Camp Croft, South Carolina, for his basic training. There, after 13 weeks of basic, they tested him on his Japanese; Sam claims it was simple hiragana and katakana readings, hardly any kanjis. He passed and soon he was on his way to Fort Snelling, Minnesota—this was in October 1945 and in December, he became a student, assigned to Company F. During mid-January 1946, however, Sam was hospitalized with a severe case of measles, which has affected his hearing to this day. Since he was out of classes for about a month, the MISLS authorities decided he would

143

Osamu (Sam) Honda

not be able to catch up with his class, so as was the practice then, he was "washed" out and assigned to Company E, the holding company for "casuals" where he did all kinds of general service jobs. Company E was dubbed the "Turkey Farm"—(the shabby five-man temporary huts, heated with a coal fed potbellied stove in the winter time did give the appearance of a large turkey farm) and it was located where the main runways face Interstate Highway 494 today. Next he was assigned to Headquarters Company for administrative work but in July 1946, as the school was transferred to the Presidio of Monterey, CA, Sam was sent to Camp Campbell, KY.

At Camp Campbell, he was placed in the Signal Corps and sent forthwith to learn the Morse Code at Fort Monmouth, NJ. The schooling at Monmouth lasted almost four months. Then Sam was sent to Fort Meade, MD where he was an instructor in signal procedures, giving extra training to those Signal Corps troops going overseas. Since Sam was within six months of his army discharge he was not selected for overseas duty.

Nearing his discharge date, the Army sent him to his home state of California; first to Camp Beale (Marysville,) where he drove a mail bus, packing a .45 caliber pistol on his hip, to pick up the Camp Beale mail bags at the Marysville Post Office. Sam was then sent to Camp Stoneman (Pittsburgh) California where he received his honorable discharge on 8 August 1946. Sam remarked that he was not a combat hero and did not receive any commendations or medals—"I was a plain good soldier who did what I was told to do and I came out a Private First Class."

Sam Resumes His Civilian Career

Realizing that California was not a Japanese friendly atmosphere during that period, and having his old job awaiting him in Cleveland, Ohio, Sam returned to his old job at Cleveland.

Like many Niseis, Sam knew that he did not want to spend his future as a blue collar industrial worker. Sam soon moved to Chicago where there were many school and job opportunities. He took advantage of the GI Bill of Rights and enrolled in night classes, first at De Paul University, and then at the Chicago Technical College. By this time Sam had married and was busy working at Chicago's Revere Camera Company.

Dame Fortune smiled on the Hondas, for the Minnesota Mining and Manufacturing Company absorbed the Revere Camera Company and transferred the Engineering Department to which Sam was assigned to Saint Paul and they settled in White Bear Lake in 1964.

Sam At 3M

At 3M Sam's value to the company steadily increased and he became a specialist of film transport designing intricate mechanisms for microfilms, projectors, and other photographic products. Sam retired in 1987, but that lasted for only a year. 3M contracted through the POSSIS Company, a temporary workers outfit, and Sam was asked to rejoin 3M. Sam, thereby, continued work at 3M for three years and six months more. Finally, Sam quit at age 65 to collect his social security.

Yet, 3M, again through POSSIS, had Sam work approximately 20 hours a week on capital equipment in the engineering division. Sam requested a lower pay scale and without any design work, nor any work that would require responsibility or work under pressure. Sam said, "I felt that I was good at what I did with the Computer Aid Design

(CAD) and so I continued with this arrangement for six years."

Sam is married to his dear wife, Lily, and they are parents of three children, Patti, Nancy, and Mark. They have a total of five grandchildren and both Sam and Lily have become invaluable grandparents and expert babysitters. Today, Sam is an inveterate golfer, and enjoys, as well, volunteering for many Nikkei and other civic programs. Lil continues being "super grandmom" as well as continuing to be the expert doll maker.

CHAPTER FIFTEEN

George Yoshino

George Yoshino was born on 25 February 1921 at Bellevue, Washington, to a family of four children. His father had a ten acre farm where he raised produce for the Seattle and other area markets. George graduated from Bellevue High School in June, 1940, and spent his prewar years helping his dad on the family farm.

The Camp Experience

When World War II commenced and with the advent of Executive Order 9066 on 19 February 1942, he and his family were post-haste moved into the Pinedale Assembly Center in Fresno, California, this was in May of 1942. His father, however, was among some of the officers of Japanese organizations who were taken into custody by the FBI. The Yoshinos were subsequently transferred to Tule Lake Camp where George held the job of a "cabinetmaker" and was paid the munificent sum of nineteen dollars per month.

In the summer of 1943, tired of camp life, George, along

with about thirty young men, volunteered to do sugar beet, as well as lettuce and potato harvesting at Caldwell, Idaho. This was the summer of 1943. After harvesting duties were com-

George Yoshiro

pleted, George returned to Tule Lake, but his next move was to work as a railroad section gang member at Missoula, Bozeman, and Butte, Montana. He, also remembers unloading lake ice into ice storage houses to be later used to replenish the railroad reefer cars and he remarked he received "really good" wages at 67 cents an hour.

George's Army Career

After his brother volunteered to join the 442nd Regimental Combat Team in March 1943, then training at Camp Shelby, Mississippi, George volunteered to join the Military Intelligence Service in August 1944. He was sent to Fort McClellan, Alabama, for his basic training and arrived in Fort Snelling, Minnesota, during Thanksgiving 1944. He graduated in August 1945, and by September he was sent to Manila, Philippine Islands.

The war ended on 15 August 1945, and so George was sent to Tokyo, as an interpreter. Like many MIS graduates, George went to ATIS (Allied Translator and Interpreter Section) which was located in the NYK (Nippon Yusen Kaisha) building in the heart of Tokyo (the Marunouchi District) and was assigned to the Documentation Section where he supervised a pool of Japanese typists. His assignments included other "office work" but the most onerous and detested duty for George was to accompany the U.S. Army's housing officer scouting for residential billets. "These homes were then occupied by our high ranking officers. I did not care for that type of duty," said George. In the meantime, in the spring of 1946 his younger brother came to Tokyo too, but he didn't stay long since he became ill and was transferred back to the states. George left Japan and received his honorable discharge in February 1947.

George received the Asiatic Pacific Ribbon, The Good Conduct Medal, and the Occupation of Japan medal and ribbon. George modestly said, "I had no so-called highlights in my service career—I was a good law abiding soldier."

George's Civilian Career

George was discharged in California but since his folks were now living in Minneapolis and a sister was in nurse's training at Red Wing, he also relocated to Minnesota. He graduated from Globe Business College in Accounting and joined Cummins and Selle, a wholesale furniture establishment and loyally worked for 40 years at Cummins and Selle's Accounting and warehousing departments, retiring in 1994. He met his wife Helen, who also worked at Cummins and Selle, and they were married in 1960. George and Helen are active members of the St. Mary's Greek Orthodox Church and the American Legion Hellenic Post 129 and its Auxiliary in Minneapolis.

CHAPTER SIXTEEN

Tom Ohno

Tom was born in Seattle, Washington, on 20 December 1927. There were ten children in the Ohno family, five boys and five girls with Tom being the fifth child. His father worked many years as a waiter in restaurants and his mother stayed at home as a homemaker. Tom attended Central and Bailey Gatzert Elementary School, Washington Junior High School, and Broadway High School for his ninth grade and the first half of his sophomore year until the Ohnos were evacuated in May of 1942.

Camp Experience

The attack on Pearl Harbor was a distinct shock to Tom and his family. Tom was seeing a film in the Orpheum Theater in Seattle when news of the attack came flashing on the screen. Lights went on and as Tom walked out to the lobby, wondering where Pearl Harbor was, angry voices shot out in the theater, "There's a Jap, Let's get him!" Frightened, Tom ran out of the theater and hurried home.

With Executive Order 9066 being proclaimed on 19 February 1942, the Ohnos were summarily hustled off to the assembly Center of Puyallup State Fair Grounds on 9 May 1942. Then sometime in August of 1942, they were sent to the Minidoka Relocation Camp, Idaho. With all the turmoil and Tom being an active youngster he refused to join the other Niseis in high school because the school made no pro-

Tom Ohno

visions for midyear students—"I goofed around for a while when they expelled me for nonattendance" Tom said. "But in September, 1943, I decided to continue my schooling and returned to the camp high school for my sophomore year."

The following year, September 1944, urged by his eldest brother Fred, Tom joined him in Minneapolis. Fred was unable to support Tom, however, so to earn his keep, Tom worked for a time as a houseboy in southwest Minneapolis, while going to school at West High School. Tom graduated from West in January of 1946. After working for a short period, Tom decided to enlist in the US Army and signed up for eighteen months.

Tom's Army Life

Tom was sent to Camp Polk, Louisiana, for his basic training and received his advanced training as a signal corps teletype repairman at Fort Monmouth, New Jersey. In order to go overseas, Tom had to extend his enlistment by six months and so, late in 1946, Tom arrived in Japan and was sent to the Allied Translator and Interpreter Section (ATIS) headquartered in the Nippon Yusen Kaisha (NYK) building in the heart of the Marunouchi Ward (business center of Tokyo) for a hurried Japanese language schooling. With increased needs for Japanese interpreter duty soldiers, Tom was sent to Korea and reported to the 6th Infantry Division headquarters, serving with their Battalion Intelligence Sections. Varied operaationes occupied his days in Korea doing claims work filed by individual Koreans as well as Korean companies against the US government. He also kept track of informants against the Korean communist members and their cells, noted and recorded the pro-USA and negative propaganda unleashed against the communists and studied the planning of any US action detrimental to the communist north. Tom worked in Seoul, Pusan and Taegu.

By October 1947, Tom was back in the USA and honorably discharged. Tom chuckled, as he recalled,

> I wanted to keep my corporal's rank and they assured me that I would be called in as a corporal should there be another war and so, I signed up for the Reserves. Well, guess what, the Korean War broke out on 25 June 1950, and I got recalled in September 1950, for one year. They sent me to Japan, this time, to do MG (military government) work in Okayama Prefecture, Japan. All in all, it was good duty, and when my year was up, the army sent me to Camp Carson, Colorado, where I received my second honorable discharge. This was September 1951.

Highlights and Awards Received By Tom

Tom considered and remarked:

> What I, at that time, may not have thought to be a highlight of my life, my recall into the Army during the Korean War, turned out to be okay. I enjoyed my time spent in Japan, and was able to visit and keep in contact with my eldest sister, who I met during my

original tour during a furlough in 1947. She and her family lived in Nobeoka City, Miyazaki Prefecture. Oh yes, I did go in as a corporal and came out of the army as a corporal.

Tom was awarded the Occupation Medals (Japan/Korea), the Good Conduct Medal, the Korean Service Medal (with three stars,) the United Nations Medal, the United Nations Service Medal, and the National Defense Service Medal.

Tom's Educational Career

Taking full advantage of his GI Bill of Rights Tom enrolled at Augsburg College in Minneapolis in the Teacher Education program. He majored in Mathematics and minored in Physical Education and received his Bachelor of Science Degree in1953. In September of that year Tom began teaching Math and Physical Education at Lincoln Junior High School. This first stint lasted four years and then he transferred his teaching to Roosevelt High School where he taught for twenty six (26) years. In 1963 he became the Junior Varsity coach of baseball at Roosevelt High School. In 1965 and on to 1970, Tom was the senior varsity coach of baseball at RHS.

Tom retired from his Minneapolis teaching duties in 1979, but the call of education was strong and so, when an opportunity arose to teach part time at Derham Hall High School in Saint Paul, Tom taught math there at the all girls school for five years more. Also, Tom went back to Roosevelt High School to coach their women's softball team. Finally, Tom retired fully from regular teaching and coaching in 1988.

In Retirement

Never one to be inactive, Tom continues to "bring the word" concerning the Japanese American experience and JA contributions to our country, focusing primarily on the detestable incarceration of Japanese Americans during World War II. Tom is a willing volunteer as a program speaker to various school classes, organizations, and groups interested in learning more about the Japanese American travails and contributions.

For the longest time Tom was the chair or cochair of the Twin Cities Japanese American Citizens League Scholarship Committee that presented monetary awards to deserving Nikkei graduates. Today he continues his work on that committee as a senior advisor. Tom was also the Twin Cities chapter president of the JACL in 1957. Tom is a strong, continuing member of the Japanese American

Veterans of Minnesota.

Tom and wife Rei are the proud parents of daughter Pam Ohno Dagobert, Robert Ohno and three grandsons. Tom and Rei enjoy ballroom dancing, taking part in physical fitness programs and love gardening when summer arrives in Minnesota.

CHAPTER SEVENTEEN

David Yahanda

Dave was born in San Francisco, California, on 31 October 1924, into a family of seven, that included his parents, two boys and three girls, he being the eldest. During his early childhood the Yahandas moved to Monterey, California, and Dave graduated from Monterey High School. His parents started a dry cleaning business in nearby Carmel.

David Yahanda

When war began the Yahandas were forced to move inland 15 miles up into Carmel Valley. Dave and his siblings commuted daily to Carmel to operate the dry cleaning business since his parents, classified as enemy aliens, were not allowed to travel. With the advent of Executive Order 9066, on the 19th of February 1942, the whole family was forced to leave Carmel soon thereafter. Dave lamented that they lost everything they had invested in the business and they could not collect a cent of the many due bills—it was a total loss.

The Camps

The Yahandas were transported by buses from their home to the Assembly Center, the Turlock County Fairgrounds. After some time spent in the Assembly Center they were moved to the Gila River Relocation Center, Arizona, by train. Dave remembers not knowing their final destination but as they passed the Salton Sea, Yuma, and finally arriving in Gila River, he realized that they had come to the hot desert country of Arizona.

They were placed in Camp Number 1 and his dad was appointed the central block manager. "Butte Camp," Dave said, "was Camp Number 2 and the camps were nothing but awful heat, dust storms and dry, dry during the day and cold, cold at night."

Dave Joins The Army

Growing very tired of the camp existence, at his first opportunity, Dave opted to go to Chicago to work. He stayed in Chicago until he was drafted in January 1945. He reported in to Fort Douglas, Utah, for induction on 8 January 1945, and was soon on his way to Fort Knox, Kentucky, for his basic training.

It was not the best of times for Dave; he was the only mainland Nisei amongst a contingent of Hawaii Niseis. It was not easy for Dave to be around Hawaii Niseis—many were flashing currency bills that relatives had sent them through the mail—they were carefree and loud as they gambled with dice, cards, and even matched coins during their free time. Dave felt left out since the Hawaiian *patois* (pidgin English) was practically incomprehensible and foreign sounding to Dave.

After basic training Dave was sent to Fort Meade, Maryland, for overseas deployment to Europe. It was at Fort Meade that he was interviewed and quizzed by several MIS NCOs (Sergeants) on his Japanese language capabilities. Happily, for Dave, he passed the test and was sent to Fort Snelling, Minnesota, immediately. At Snelling, Dave studied hard and graduated in the spring of 1945. Dave was ticketed to go to the Pacific theater when illness overtook him and he was left behind at Snelling as his classmates went overseas for Pacific theater assignments.

When Dave returned to duty he was assigned to Headquarters Company, where he joined Bill Doi, another present member of Japanese American Veterans Minnesota. Dave then helped move the Military Intelligence Service

Language School to Presidio of Monterey, California, which is now known as the Defense Language Institute.

Discharge and Civilian Life in Minnesota

Dave then received his honorable discharge at Fort Ord, California, receiving the WWII Victory medal, good conduct medal and other service ribbons. Dave remarked, "I did my duty as an American and soldiered the best I could...I was a good soldier."

Instead of staying in California, since the family was already located in the Twin Cities, his father having taught Japanese in the Army Specialized Training Program, Dave decided to return to Minnesota. He soon found employment and retired in Minnesota. He and his wife, Ruth love the Minnesota outdoors and Dave is an avowed fisherman, fishing all year round.

CHAPTER EIGHTEEN

Conclusion

The Japanese American Veterans Minnesota is a community oriented social as well as a veterans organization. Its members, sparse in numbers, have carried out its objectives in the following ways. They have been asked by the local Japanese American community, especially the Twin Cities Chapter of the Japanese American Citizens League, to add the patriotic and educational features to their programs and we have responded.

Be it the posting of flags at formal gatherings, providing guest speakers and resource personnel to enhance the programs in schools, colleges, clubs, church organizations, chambers of commerce, radio and television stations, newspapers, historical societies, and many more. We have been there to educate the unknowing public. This organization has served well the Japanese American community in explaining and retelling the tragic story of the incarceration of Japanese Americans of World War II and the brave actions of the Nisei soldiers in winning a place in America for all those with Japanese ethnicity.

We have provided historical Japanese American exhibits, have composed and read professional papers and published books extolling the contributions of the Nikkei citizens to the greatness of America. We hosted a national Japanese American Veterans Reunion, and continue to memorialize our JA veterans in a public memorial service at Fort Snelling National Cemetery.

As time goes by our ranks continue to shrink—we have but thirty three members at this writing. In other locales, the sons and daughters have stepped in to continue the ongoing work of the veterans. We hope that this will occur here in Minnesota. We have a good start in our indispensable Secretary Treasurer, Kathy Ohama Koch.

A final word, in the form of a note of keen appreciation to the spouses and widows of our veterans. Without their support as associate members and providers of the tasty and plentiful *gochiso* (food), JAVM could not be a continuing success. Thank you ladies.

OTHER JAVM MEMBERS

Bill Doi-MISLS (Army)

John Takekawa-Army Vet

Jim Kirihara-Army Vet

Jim Murakami-Army

Dean Yanari

Frank Yanari

Nobuo Kimura-442nd RCT

Yuki Akaki-442nd RCT

CAMP SAVAGE, WINTER, 1942

CAMP SAVAGE

During World War II, some 5,000-6,000 Japanese American soldiers, members of the U. S. Army's Military Intelligence Service, were given intensive and accelerated classes in the Japanese language at Camp Savage.

Their subsequent work translating captured documents, maps, battle plans, diaries, letters, and printed materials and interrogating Japanese prisoners made them "Our human secret weapons," according to President Harry Truman, who commended them following the war.

The Military Intelligence Service (MIS) program began in the fall of 1941, a few weeks before Pearl Harbor, at the Presidio in San Francisco.

For security reasons it was moved in May, 1942 to Camp Savage, a site personally selected by language school commandant Colonel Kai E. Rasmussen, who believed Savage was "a community that would accept Japanese Americans for their true worth -- American soldiers fighting with their brains for their native America."

The 132-acre site had served as a Civilian Conservation Corps camp in the 1930s and was later used to house elderly indigent men.

Conditions there were extremely difficult in the early months of the war, when the first students studied without desks, chairs, or even beds. By August, 1944 the program had outgrown Camp Savage and was moved to larger facilities at Fort Snelling.

Most of the English-speaking Japanese Americans, known as Nisei, were from the West Coast area. Some were already in the U.S. military service when they were selected for the language school, while others were volunteers from the camps in which American citizens of Japanese ancestry had been interned following the bombing of Pearl Harbor.

According to General Charles Willoughby, chief of intelligence for General Douglas MacArthur, "the 6,000 Nisei shortened the Pacific war by two years."

ERECTED BY THE
SAVAGE CHAMBER OF COMMERCE
1993

The Camp Savage memorial monument

OLD FORT SNELLING

The old field house—Many dances were held here

The old PX and snack bar were located here

The old parade ground, now a golf course

The old polo field, now an athletic field

The old classroom buildings, now in
disrepair and abandoned

Rear view of old classroom buildings

The old Fort Snelling Headquarters building,
now boarded up

The old headquarters of the
Military Intelligence Language School

The old bachelor officer's building

Old time spacious officer's homes, now in disrepair

JAVM MEETINGS/LUNCHEONS

From left to right, Dr. George Tani, Tosh Abe
and Yosh Matsumoto

Mits Yoneji (left) and Isamu Saito

JAVM MEMORIAL DAY SERVICE

Sam Honda, Chair of Memorial
Service, welcoming all

U.S. Army Chaplain K Beale
led Veteran's Memorial Service

JAVM honoring deceased Nikkei vets at
Fort Snelling National Cemetery

Spouses, widows, relatives and friends
came to honor deceased vets